HOW TO THINK LIKE A
SURVIVOR

A Guide for Wilderness Emergencies

Tom Watson

**Creative Publishing
international**

Chanhassen, Minnesota

DEDICATION

To my dad, who started me off on my first
steps outdoors; to my mother and sister for
surviving my crazy adventures all these years and
whose love and support show no bounds.

**Creative Publishing
international**

Copyright © 2006 by Creative Publishing international, Inc.
18705 Lake Drive East
Chanhassen, MN 55317
1-800-328-3895
www.creativepub.com

President/CEO: Ken Fund
Vice President/Publisher: Linda Ball
Vice President/Retail Sales & Marketing: Kevin Haas
Executive Editor, Outdoor Group: Barbara Harold
Creative Director: Brad Springer
Page Design & Layout: Linda Siegel
Project Manager: Tracy Stanley
Production Manager: Laura Hokkanen

Printed on American paper by R. R. Donnelley
10 9 8 7 6 5 4 3 2 1

How to Think Like a Survivor
by Tom Watson

Front Cover Photos: © 2006 Mitch Kezar/Windigo Images (top and
   bottom right); Creative Publishing international (bottom left)
Illustrations by: Ron Carboni

Library of Congress Cataloging-in-Publication Data
Watson, Tom
  How to think like a survivor : a guide for wilderness emergencies
  / by Tom Watson.
    p. cm.
  Includes index.
  ISBN 1-58923-217-8 (soft cover)
  1. Wilderness survival--Handbooks, manuals, etc. 2. Survival
skills--Handbooks, manuals, etc. I. Title.
  GV200.5.W38 2005
  613.6'9--dc22   2005002785

Table of Contents

Introduction **4**

Chapter 1 ....**6**
Elements of Survival

Chapter 2.. **14**
Assessing the Survival Mode

Chapter 3 .... **28**
Overview of Personal Gear

Chapter 4 .... **54**
The Importance of Shelter

Chapter 5 .... **74**
Finding Water

Chapter 6 .... **88**
Searching for Food

Chapter 7 .... **102**
Building a Fire

Chapter 8 .... **120**
Making Signals

Chapter 9 .... **136**
Developing Navigation Skills

Chapter 10 .... **146**
Field First Aid and Natural Remedies

Appendix... **180**
    Components of a Survival Kit
    Lost on the Moon Test
    Further Reading

Author Acknowledgments **188**

Index **189**

INTRODUCTION

Being a "survivor" in the real world is nothing like the manipulated, contrived game-show connotation so many may associate with that term. Surviving a true life-threatening situation in the outdoors is a serious, often traumatic event that can call upon human reserves many of us may not even know we have. Survival is not a game. It's using whatever means possible to stay alive in a situation where most or all of our common comforts and expected resources are denied us.

This book is not, as many survival books seem to be, just another cookie-cutter primer of the same old military survivor techniques. You are not going to be shown fifteen different ways to trap a rabbit, or read a botanical listing of every plant ever considered "edible" and all the other collections of know-how that clutters up the pages of so many survival books.

Rather, this book hopes to prepare you mentally for dealing with any survival situation by helping you think like a survivor beforehand. A survival situation is a uniquely trying experience. What may be a walk-in-the-park for one person can pit another against life-threatening challenges. Each of us may be required to face a situation in which we must become self-reliant, where common sense, a few basic skills and, most importantly, the will to live, will be the key elements in making us a survivor in the true sense.

Life lessons are often the most difficult to endure, especially when the course is hard and unforgiving. It's learning from those incidents that helps us become more aware of what can go wrong, what we still need to learn and, most importantly, what we can do to be better prepared to prevent a "next time" from ever happening again.

The all-too-common scenario is this: A marginally equipped group with limited experience goes out to enjoy an activity such as hunting, fishing or boating, and something happens that is totally unexpected and for which they are sorely underprepared. In nearly 95 percent of all survival scenarios, rescue happens within 72 hours of the initial report.

How can you prepare for such an incident? What are the physical and mental challenges that victims may surely face when thrown into a survival situation? What kinds of preparations and preventative measures can you take to at least minimize a survival situation? One way is to begin thinking like a survivor. Begin by focusing on your under-standing, prepara-tion and training and practice of outdoor survival skills. Most important-ly, develop yourself mentally.

One of the best tools available to us in a survival situation is right between our ears. Our minds, our mental state, can be the one factor that determines whether we are rescued—or recov-ered in a body bag.

POSITIVE MENTAL ATTITUDE

The mental or psychological aspects of survival immediately come into play in almost any survival situation. That's why, to their credit, so many books on survival refer to the phrase: "Positive Mental Attitude." It is most commonly referenced throughout survival discussions by its abbreviation, PMA. Positive mental attitude sums up the defining factors that will ultimately save your life: a positive approach to the situation at hand by being prepared, being mentally aware, and constantly maintaining an attitude of survival, in yourself, and quite possibly as a moti-vation to others.

PMA reaches far beyond the best survival gear, the most advanced training and the farthest reaches of Lady Luck. Some survivors may not know what PMA means, but it was probably what contributed to their survival. They just never gave up, they had the will to live, an attitude that they were going to live to tell about it no matter how severe or hopeless the present situation seemed to be. This is at the core of all survival training—no matter what happens, don't give up.

Developing and maintaining PMA is vital for surviving. Dealing with the physical elements of survival is a matter of prepared-ness as well. Learning how to improvise and being able to see the multiple utility in everything around you can be life-saving skills. Anticipating problems, no matter how large or small, and having solutions ahead of time, are other important parts of being prepared.

Learning to prioritize tasks can save your life. Do you make a fire before constructing that lean-to? Maybe not, especially if a storm is imminent and all your gear is still dry. By thinking like a survivor, you learn how to become better prepared. By being prepared, you become a more skilled survivor—and hopefully a more proficient, responsible and appreciative user of our great outdoors.

Chapter 1

Elements of Survival

Surviving an emergency situation should not be a random series of acts that hopefully come together to produce results—namely, your rescue. Steps to surviving are most effective if they are developed and completed in order of priority.

Having the discipline to execute those priorities in order is being a survivor. Learning basic skills, calling upon a list of priorities and routinely reassessing those priorities all contribute to a sound regimen that can save your life.

shelter

food

water

PRIORITIZING IS THE KEY

In a nutshell, here is my plan of action for anyone in an emergency situation:

The first priority is removing yourself and others from any immediate or pending hazards. For instance: Is the plane you crashed in about to explode? Will the beach you reached after capsizing be underwater at high tide? And so on.

Once that immediate threat is past, it's time to kick your

survival sense into action. Here are some examples of questions you should ask yourself:

➤ Are there any injuries to yourself or members of your party?
➤ What protection can you provide against the elements?
➤ Do you have access to water?
➤ Do you have enough food?
➤ How can you make it easier for someone to find you?
➤ What can you do mentally to be a survivor?

All the tasks necessary to answer each of these questions is what survival training is all about. What to do to accomplish each step of each task will depend on what resources you have, either in preparation for this incident or that you can improvise along the way. The key to most survival situations is having a working plan of action.

After ensuring immediate safety, there are three levels of action to accomplish in a survival situation:

➤ First, assess the physical well-being of the group. If your predicament was caused by an accident, injuries need to be determined and treated. Injuries may be discovered right away or may take time to manifest themselves (some internal injuries, for example). A good leader looks for early signs of hypothermia. Shivering is the obvious one, but a gradual loss of coordination and slurred speech are other signs. The physical condition of each member should be checked periodically.

One "trick" used in sea kayaking to determine if a paddler is becoming hypothermic is to drop back and paddle behind the presumed victim and see if he or she is able to maintain an even, steady course. Slight drifting and side slipping could mean the paddler is having problems. Always err on the side of prevention in such cases—stop what you are doing and take action to provide proper warmth to the victim.

➤ Second, monitor the mental and emotional well-being of the group.

➤ Third, perform a resource assessment. Remember potential water sources or useful types of vegetation that may come in handy later on. Sometimes the immediate area becomes exhausted of resources and your group may have to move on. Reassessing a new camp will be a priority. Ask questions like these: How long can this new location sustain us? How visible is this new location to rescuers? If weather worsens, are we safe here?

Again, there will be many things to think about and actions to take. Having priorities will help you make the best decisions.

SEVEN STEPS TO SURVIVAL
A good way to start thinking like a survivor is to become familiar with the Alaska Marine Safety Institute's "Seven Steps to Survival." They were developed as part of the training programs conducted for the U.S. Coast Guard and members of Alaska's commercial fishing industry. Considering each component in the following order will help you prioritize your thinking in your particular emergency situation.

1. **Awareness:** Know you are in a very serious, potentially life-threatening situation and start your survival mode immediately. Accept the situation, gain your composure and kick it in gear—get that positive mental attitude focused on your survival.

2. **Inventory:** First, conduct an inventory of your surroundings to assess any dangers—those related to the incident (gas igniting from a plane crash, for

example), or the need for a more protected area for immediate shelter (tide rising on a narrow beach on which you just capsized). Next, make an inventory of all injuries, starting with your own. Once those injuries are assessed and treated, it's time to make an inventory of the area around you for any materials you can use for your survival. Is there a source of water nearby? Are there materials lying around that could be used to construct a shelter? Are there any potential hazards that need to be dealt with? What kind of signals will work best in this area? Make a quick, mental inventory of what is at your disposal. As you proceed through the seven steps, you have a good idea of what resources are available to you.

An important aspect of the inventory step is to dismiss nothing as useless. A couple of feet (60 cm) of 1-inch-diameter (2.5-cm) rope may seem almost comically too short, but what if you were to separate those strands into thinner sections and join them into cordage for lashing or thread for sewing?

3. **Shelter:** This is the second most important step (after assessing and treating injuries). Inventory assessment (step 2) is really an intermittent step that could be accomplished in conjunction with finding materials to make a shelter since you are also assessing what materials (for tools and construction) are available to help you complete tasks. It is important to find or make a suitable shelter as soon as possible so the condition of each member of the survival group does not deteriorate due to lowering temperatures, wet conditions and so on. At least a temporary shelter will protect you from the elements as you guard against hypothermia. You can always reassess your shelter as you go over and update your survival steps each day (always monitor your situation by going through the list as many times as necessary).

4. Signals: In many regions of the country, even remote areas of Alaska, there are routine and scheduled traveling routes taken by commuter airplanes, fishing and charter boats and others in transit, for business or pleasure. Signaling to one of these passersby as soon as possible may mean the difference between a few hours of anxiety and a night of surviving before help arrives. If your party is big enough, split duties and let some pursue this step while others continue with water and food. If you are alone, your knowledge of local routines will be a factor in what you decide to do.

5. Water: Find it, collect it, purify it and drink it to stay healthy. Focus on finding a source of drinking water within the next two days. Use a piece of plastic to form a basin to collect rain water or find a nearby stream. Perhaps as part of your shelter you can rig up a water-collecting system.

6. Eat/Food: You can go a really long time without food. Sadly, as Americans get fatter, that obesity could actually save someone by calling upon those reserves in a survival situation. There are natural foods you can learn to identify, gather and process in addition to being prepared by having food with you. Once hunger pangs subside (after 18-24 hours generally), most survivors can go quite a while without additional sustenance.

7. Play/Stress relief: Surviving is a stressful situation. It demands disciplining yourself with confidence-building positive mental attitude (PMA). Some form of play or rest relaxes the mind and can ease anxiety. It is a very crucial step on the list. In group situations, fear can feed upon fear, so instilling confidence and reassurances is a key role in keeping everyone a survivor instead of becoming a fatality. Making a task part of a game—who can collect the most grass to soften up a bed, or who can gather the most firewood—can serve two important needs at once.

Any memory trick to help you recall particular sequences of events is helpful, especially under the stress of a survival situation. An easy way to help you remember these steps in order is the acronym KISSWEP: Know/realize, Inventory, Shelter, Signal, Water, Eat/food, Play.

NINE RULES OF SURVIVAL

Next, you will need to know the proper steps to take if you become lost. The Search and Rescue Society of British Columbia has established the "Nine Rules of Survival," rules for adults and children in the event they become lost in the woods. It is important to teach these rules to youngsters and to assure them that being lost is no reason to be ashamed or punished. I find these rules a good reinforcement of many of the concepts discussed throughout this book.

1. **Stay together.** Use each other to stay warm even if the "other" is a friend or just a pet. Snuggling together optimizes body heat and encourages a group to stay put.

2. **Don't wander.** Sometimes called the "hug a tree" concept, it teaches kids—and adults—about staying in one place to make search and rescue efforts easier and faster. Assure children that people will be looking for them and the best action they can take is to stay put in a safe place.

3. **Keep warm.** Watch what the animals do; they gather grass and leaves together and crawl inside. Stuff your clothes with warm, soft grasses and wear your hat! It's important to stay warm.

4. **Do not hide.** Find a safe, comfortable place out of the weather but be sure not to hide from the people who are looking for you.

5. Wear something bright. If you have an extra-large piece of bright clothing that you're not wearing, or maybe a brightly colored tarp or even some hair ribbon, hang it near where you are waiting so rescuers can spot it.

6. Try to look big for searchers. Find your waiting place next to a large open field and be ready to run out and wave if you hear an airplane overhead. Even if the ground is cold and there is no snow, you can lie down and pretend you are making snow angels. (If there is snow, don't lie on the cold ground any longer than you have to.) Also, do not try to follow the noise. Remember rule 2: Don't wander.

7. Don't lie on bare ground. Except for signaling, don't lie directly on the ground. Your body will lose too much heat. Animals use leaves and grasses to make a soft bed; you should do the same.

8. Don't eat unknown things. It's hard to not eat anything with your stomach growling, but hang on—those feelings usually fade after about 18 hours. If you are absolutely sure what the food is, go ahead and eat a little bit of it.

9. Find water to drink, but stay away from lakes and rivers. The risk of falling into a lake or river is not worth quenching your thirst. Instead, find a small puddle of water or a shallow place where you can get water without the fear of falling in and drowning. If there is dew on the leaves in the morning, gather a bunch in your hand and squeeze the water into your mouth like drinking from a sponge.

SPECIAL TIPS FOR CHILDREN

Everyone in your outing group, especially children, should be given a whistle and taught that it is an emergency signaling device and not a toy. Teach everyone that two quick blasts should be used to help locate others out of sight, and three loud blasts in a row is the signal for help. Make sure each person has at least one whistle on a lanyard, ready for use.

An easy-to-make survival kit that children can carry in their pockets on all outings contains a whistle, a small LED flashlight and a sturdy garbage bag that can be used as an emergency poncho or shelter. If your child is old enough, perhaps include a lighter or teach him or her how to use one of the flint/spark fire starters. These and a few other items can be placed in the child's fanny pack. Be sure to stress that the pack must be carried with them at all times during the outing.

Children should learn about diseases that come from drinking contaminated water. However, as for adults, perhaps it is better to treat dehydration immediately and risk contracting something several weeks later—your call.

A survival kit that will be actually used by children (and adults!) must pass three tests:

➤ It must be small enough that carrying it with you is not even a second thought, as automatic as putting on your underwear! This means lightweight and compact.

➤ Each item should be multipurpose and essential. Even the container can be used as a signal (if shiny and metallic), a small water container or a small pot in which to sterilize water or cook.

➤ It must be carried with the person at all times! As a kayaker, I saw too many of my paddling buddies secure their survival kits behind their seats or tape them to the underside of their deck. What good would those do if they capsized and lost their boat? Make up a small waterproof fanny pack or other pouch and simply don't leave home—or camp—without it!

Chapter 2

Assessing the Survival Mode

How well you succeed at being a survivor can depend on how well you are prepared—both before the incident and during the arduous, possibly painful and unforgiving process of surviving. Besides the incident itself, other factors will affect your survival. Weather, terrain, mechanical failures, even human factors will play into whatever predicament you're in. Knowing what to anticipate from each of those elements is a first step in preparing to be a survivor.

CIRCUMSTANCES

Does it really matter what led to the point where your adventure becomes a predicament and that predicament becomes a survival situation? Probably not, but being forewarned means being forearmed. As experience grows, so should your awareness of potential scenarios so you can plan accordingly.

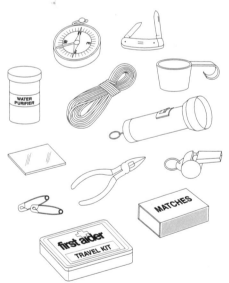

You may have ample gear and supplies, but become

hopelessly lost. You may know exactly where you are but because of an accident or mechanical failure, you are unable to proceed or call for assistance. You may be totally under-equipped for the circumstances that have suddenly appeared and have only minimal gear for that day and the next, if you are lucky.

Knowing what elements you may face can help you prepare yourself. Will I need a compass? Will it be cold? Are my boots good enough for the likely terrain?

Worst of all, you or a member of your party may become ill or injured. Having those challenges to deal with—yours or others—immediately increases the severity of any survival situation by a notch or two.

Survival Tip: Broken Wrist Challenge

Do you feel pretty confident that you can tend to a survival task with ease? Here's a demonstration of what happens when you throw an injury into a task as simple as lighting a match to start a fire.

Take a 3- to 4-inch-wide (7- to 10-cm) elastic bandage and push three or four thumb tacks through the cloth near one end of the strip in a cluster pattern. Carefully lay the bandage across your wrist and lower hand with the points of the tacks resting painlessly against your skin.

Next, carefully wrap the bandage around your wrist a few times. It should be snug and gently pressing the points of the tacks against your skin, but not cause any pain, just a tingling, perhaps.

Secure the end of the bandage and attempt to complete the simple task of lighting a match. Just trying to bend your wrist will force the tack tips into your skin producing pain that can mimic a broken wrist or hand.

Imagine if it's your "good" hand. See how cumbersome, slow and painful that simple task has become?

Being prepared and anticipating potential emergencies is a far better mode to maintain than trying to endure an incident that takes you by surprise. Even experts can get blind-sided, but preventative measures are always preferred over curative ones. These are the lessons learned that also give a person a higher level of confidence and a broader foundation for that critical positive mental attitude.

Mechanical or Equipment Failures

These unforeseen malfunctions are often what instantly put people right smack into the middle of a survival situation. Motors burn out, engines stall, things just quit working, you leave some vital piece of equipment at home. Your vehicle should be equipped with blankets, water, food and signaling devices. There's plenty of room to also keep a first aid kit tucked into the back corner of the trunk. Thinking like a survivor may mean you anticipate certain breakdowns and you carry an extra engine belt and the tools to replace it. There might be other spare parts you can and should carry.

Survival Tip: The Versatile Nylon Stocking

Many years ago, a popular emergency item suggested for cars was an old nylon stocking. It could be tied into a loop and used as an emergency fan belt. Whether or not this makeshift belt would work on newer engines, I don't know. I do know, however, that the stocking also works as cordage for lashing, holding compresses on a wound, catching fish or bait, and filtering water. It also makes a handy soap container and scrubbing surface, for hanging soap to dry, for storage and for keeping bits of litter from sticking to the soap when you drop it on the ground.

Weather

More often than not, weather is a major contributing factor in survival situations. Hypothermia is the number-one killer and can be brought about by nothing more than a drop in air temperature below 70°F (21°C). Cloud cover can obscure the sun so your direction of travel becomes unclear. Rain-drenched gear can malfunction, and damp bodies begin to cool. In many aircraft crashes weather is a contributing factor, even though the accident is officially attributed to pilot error. Fog cover can be deadly and can both crop up suddenly and seem to linger forever.

Weather can be a good element, too. Clouds mean protection from the sun (but not UV rays) in the desert, and rainwater means you won't go thirsty.

Layering the proper clothing and wearing a proper shell are two measures you can take to be prepared. There is no such thing as bad weather, just bad clothing!

Know how to read the weather. By that I mean be familiar with what different cloud covers indicate, the amount and frequency of a rise or fall in the barometric pressure in your region, the character of the prevailing winds throughout the day and anticipated or unexpected temperature changes. These are all potential contributing factors leading up to and then affecting your survival mode.

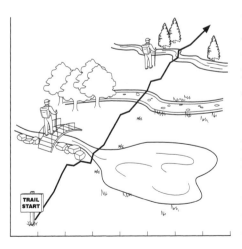

Geography

A prudent outdoor enthusiast takes precautions before going into a particular environment. While there are basic precautions and preparations regardless of destination, each environment offers its own challenges:

➤ Deserts automatically raise the issue of the availability and consumption of water (although hydration is critical in all environments), as well as adequate shelter from the heat.

➤ In the Far North, the sheer vastness of areas, severe temperature changes and scant resources pose special challenges.

➤ In mountainous country and along coasts, particularly, it is critical to anticipate increases in elevation.

Unknown geography can confuse travelers to the point of complete disorientation. Unfamiliar terrain can invite human error and suffering. Ill-fitting boots on unforgiving terrain can cause blisters that get infected, sprained ankles or worse.

Preparations based on the geography of an area include utilizing current and appropriate maps. You will need to select appropriate clothing and have the proper gear (commercial or makeshift) along with the skills to use them. You should also be aware of situations elsewhere that might affect you in the very near future.

For instance, washes and gullies in the desert offer alluring shady places out of the unforgiving sun. Often the floor of the draw or wash is flat, making it a very tempting place to set up camp. However, these washes are notorious for catching campers and hikers off guard when rain surges down these channels flushing everything along with it. Advancing to higher ground is the common practice, usually at the onset of a major downpour. What's equally important, however, is to be aware of rain falling many miles away. While you are enjoying blue skies, a deluge farther up the canyon may already be channeling a torrent of water toward you.

EMOTIONS

The incident that puts a person into the survival mode and its resulting damage or injuries are the tangible aspects of the survival mode. Equally important and just as devastating can be the emotional challenge faced by victims. These psychological elements are intangible.

In First Responder: A Skills Approach, authors Keith J. Karren and Brent Q. Hafen discuss psychological emergencies, and stress the importance of acknowledging the human factors in such emergencies:

➤ Humans have limitations; we are all susceptible to emotional injury, including the person in charge or in the leadership role.

➤ We all have a right to (and need for) our own feelings. We are all going to react differently, based on many factors. We must accept our emotions and others' emotions as natural and offer care, as we are able.

➤ Behind almost every emotional manifestation is strength in some form. Humans are incredibly resilient—we have the will to live!

➤ Everyone is going to feel some emotional disturbance over an injury. Imagine the emotions of a dancer who has just suffered a severe ankle injury and realizes that help is not immediately available.

➤ Emotional injury is just as real as physical injury.

Recognizing these psychological elements and addressing them individually will be a key challenge in successfully surviving an ordeal, especially one involving even a small number of people. Here are some of the most common emotions that are manifested in emergency situations:

Anxiety

This emotion is usually directly associated with an identifiable threat. We all tend to harbor a bit more anxiety outside the protective walls of our homes. So it should be no surprise that the strange and threatening surroundings of the outdoors can bring that suppressed anxiety to the surface immediately.

Physically, anxiety can cause a rise in diastolic blood pressure. A person's heart may beat faster, and he or she may experience shallow breathing. Hyperventilation, sweating, vomiting and chills are all physical symptoms of anxiety. A person who is diabetic may experience a rise in blood sugars. Severe anxiety can be the springboard for fear and panic attacks.

Survival Tip: **Known Medical Conditions**

Members of your party who have an imposing medical condition should share that information with the others. They should include information about any medications and dosages they have with them. This should be written down with any other pertinent information and kept where all can refer to it if necessary.

Reassurances about the immediate situation and other forms of comforting can help ease anxiety. Physical exercise can have an ameliorating affect on anxiety as well as provide a mechanism for generating warmth. Be advised, however, that aerobic exercise (e.g., jogging) is less stressful on the body and uses less energy to generate that warmth than anaerobic exercise (e.g., push ups).

Fear

It's a common feeling we have all had to overcome at one time or another. Fear can help keep our guard up, keep us alert, push us to the max. Some people suffer from phobias, which are unrealistic or illogical fears. Hippocrates, the Father of Medicine, is said to have suffered from aulophobia, fear of the flute! Agoraphobia, the fear of strange places, challenges many people.

More to the point of survival, fear can bring anxiety to higher levels and affect judgment and actions. Physically, fear can cause the pulse to quicken, pupils to dilate and perspiration to form on hands and feet. It can also cause nausea and vomiting. Fear can create situations that warrant immediate attention. Sweating, for example, means a body is losing heat—not a good situation when hypothermia is the cause of death in most survival situations.

Fortunately, a person's fear can usually be overcome by encouraging him or her to accomplish a manageable task. As a leader in a survival situation, you may have to come up with ways to get a companion's mind off whatever fears he or she may have.

Panic Attack
Having someone succumb to a panic attack is not an unrealistic concern. Caused by a recognizable stress situation, panic attacks can cause victims to experience numbness or tingling of their hands and face, especially around their lips.

Other symptoms include shaking, heart palpitations, sweating, chest pains and a feeling of smothering or choking.

If you think these sound similar to signs of a heart attack, you are correct. This is a tough call, but victims of panic attacks may have had them before, sometimes as many as three or four times. Getting this information from them or someone who knows their history can at least give you some reassurance that it is not a heart attack.

One of the best ways to aid a person suffering from a
panic attack is to make reassuring, positive adjustments
to the overall situation. Meditation and aerobic exercises
have also proven beneficial in comforting panic attack
victims. Generally, these attacks subside in 15 to 20
minutes.

Survival Tip: **Herbal Therapies**

One treatment suggested for anxiety and panic attack is a tea
made from the flowers of chamomile (lemon balm) or linden
(basswood) trees. It acts as a mild relaxant and tranquilizer.
Warning: Some people have a severe allergic reaction to
chamomile tea that causes their throat to swell, severely
restricting airflow. If the victim has never had chamomile, try a
small sip first to detect any negative reaction. Or, better yet, try
another remedy, just to be safe!

Depression

Depression is a normal reaction to an event or situation.
It is important to remember that "event depression" is not
a sign of emotional weakness.

Depression is the most common psychological problem in
the United States today. It is estimated that 25 percent of
the women and 10 percent of the men in the world suffer
from some degree of depression. It's only natural that this
emotion will kick in during a survival situation, clearly
jeopardizing the focus of the group and being counter-
productive to any PMA generated.

Depression shows itself in several forms, including sad-
ness, pessimism, guilt and worthlessness. It also makes it
hard for the victim to concentrate. It causes fatigue,
anxiety and loss of interest.

Fortunately, most of a person's depression can be reversed. First and foremost is to acknowledge that it's OK to have those feelings—being sad is a natural emotion. Sharing feelings about the situation can help. Help the depressed person to talk about the problem, and listen with sincerity and understanding. Do not try to minimize the person's concerns or deny the severity of a situation. Rather, talk through solutions. A depressed person is not in the best decision-making mode, but providing the person with alternative situations to deal with will get his or her mind off the main problem.

Some experts suggest a good group cry, and then, once the tears have fallen—move on! Start that PMA process and continue forward. Your life or the lives of others probably depend upon it.

Exercise is another effective way of countering or reducing depression.

Survival Tip: **Depression Relief**

Vitamin B6 is often cited as a possible aid to alleviate depression. It is available as pyridoxine and is found naturally in lean meats, brown rice, whole grains and nuts.

Guilt

The human mind can conjure up a Pandora's box of emotions and mental interference in a survival situation. A victim may feel guilty because he or she has put others at risk. One challenge search and rescue (SAR) teams have in finding young victims is that children often feel guilty about being lost and are afraid of punishment; therefore, they actually hide from searchers.

Ego and the fear of being ridiculed are also present in some survival situations. One of our SAR missions in

Kodiak involved an Asian tourist whose grandfather was a famous tiger hunter in his home country. The grandson wandered away from the remote resort one afternoon and spent two days criss-crossing the forested island. At the end of our first full day of searching, the young man simply wandered back into camp—finding it by blind luck—and returned to his cabin. We later learned that he had become disoriented but was embarrassed because his grandfather had been such an accomplished outdoorsman.

Stress

The way you react to a situation can cause stress. How you perceive that situation can determine the level of stress you feel. Stress is what triggers the human "fight or flight" response. It is our biochemical reaction to danger. Our heart pumps faster, blood pressure rises and our brain redirects blood to our muscles for extra strength. Unfortunately, this blood is taken from other parts of our body, including our digestive and immune systems. Constantly rerouting that blood supply can lead to problems in the long haul.

Some stress-related symptoms include:

➤ Dizzy spells or blackouts
➤ A racing pulse that won't stop
➤ Sweaty palms
➤ Chronic back and/or neck pain
➤ Severe headaches
➤ Trembling
➤ Hives
➤ Overwhelming anxiety
➤ Insomnia

Unless stress can be released or significantly diminished,

it can lead to hypertension. As the body's resources are depleted, stress can lead to chronic fatigue as well. As simple as it sounds, one of the best remedies for alleviating stress is getting the sufferer's mind off the stressful situation. A sense of being in control can be an answer. Again, encouraging victims to have a positive mental attitude and helping them find a way to focus on a positive solution are major remedies for dealing with stress. Another cure that seems to work is a primordial release in the form of a good scream. If it's timed right, maybe the rescuers will hear it as well!

Other ways to alleviate stress include having the victim become involved in one of the survival tasks you identify. Concentrating on collecting firewood or building a better fire or shelter can help the person focus on the specific task instead of the overall stressful situation.

Vigorous aerobic exercise is effective in reducing stress as it reduces certain hormone levels in the body.

Fatigue
A stressful, emotionally charged survival situation will be physically challenging as well, to the point the victim becomes exhausted, worn out, dead tired. Exerting energy that is not readily replaced leads to fatigue. One reason for not continuing forth when lost is that you are spending energy on an unknown or questionable outcome. Save that energy by stopping and thinking through your options.

Exercise can actually stimulate energy, more so if that exercise becomes a routine. Remember, however, that too much strenuous exercise has a depleting effect and can cause perspiration, which evaporates the warmth you've just built up. It's all a matter of balance.

Anger

An extension of several of these emotions is anger. It can be focused toward a person blamed for the mishap or it may mask the guilt one has for feeling responsible for the incident. Anger can be very disruptive and non-productive. As a leader you must try to subdue it in your group.

MIND AIDS

The mental or psychological aspects of survival immed-iately come into play in almost any survival situation. That's why, to their credit, so many books on survival refer to the phrase: "Positive Mental Attitude." It is most commonly referenced throughout survival discussions as its abbreviation: PMA. Positive mental attitude sums up the defining factors that will ultimately save your life: a positive approach to the situation at hand by being prepared, being mentally aware, and constantly main-taining an attitude of survival, in yourself, and quite possibly as a motivation to others.

PMA reaches far beyond the best survival gear, the most advanced training and the farthest reaches of Lady Luck. Some survivors may not know what PMA means, but it was probably what contributed to their survival. They just never gave up, they had the will to live, an attitude that they were going to live to tell about it no matter how severe or hopeless the present situation seemed to be. This is at the core of all survival training—no matter what happens, don't give up. Developing and maintaining PMA is vital for surviving.

Dealing with the physical elements of survival is a matter of preparedness as well. Learning how to improvise and being able to see the multiple utility in everything around you can be life-saving skills. Anticipating problems, no matter how large or small, and having solutions ahead of time, are other important parts of being prepared.

Learning to prioritize tasks can save your life. Do you make a fire before constructing that lean-to? Maybe not, especially if a storm is imminent and all your gear is still dry. By thinking like a survivor, you learn how to become better prepared. By being prepared, you become a more skilled survivor—and hopefully a more proficient, responsible and appreciative user of our great outdoors.

Chapter 3

Overview of Personal Gear

Before we even get into survival clothing and gear, I want you to take a test. Don't look up the answers (in Appendix II) until you've finished reading this book because you should take this same test again. You can then compare your "before" and "after" answers to see if you have a different perspective on prioritizing survival gear. Good luck—and don't peek!

The "Lost on the Moon Test" surfaced at the height of NASA's Apollo program. Supposedly it was a test given as part of the astronaut-training program to determine the level of survival instincts astronauts had. It's good exercise to see where your thought process takes you as you read through the options. Even if you are not space savvy, take the test and check the results to see the reasoning behind the ranking of each item. It will give you an idea of how thinking like a survivor can apply to many different situations.

CLOTHING

What you have for gear—starting with the clothes on your back—can be a key factor that could bring on a survival situation or, hopefully, reduce the severity of one. That said, there are documented cases where having proper gear, but not using it correctly or soon enough, has had tragic consequences. Clothing plays a critical role because a significant or continuing loss of body warmth will most assuredly lead to hypothermia. Once hypothermia sets in, chances of survival diminish if not treated promptly.

There was a case of a lost hunter whose body was ultimately found within 100 yards (91 m) of a moderately traveled county road. He had walked the last quarter mile (0.4 km) through knee-deep snow in subfreezing weather wearing only his underwear. SAR members retraced his tracks and found his empty pack sitting in the snow. Each

item of clothing (warm sweaters, extra layers, etc.) was folded and stacked neatly beside it. Tragically, the victim may have thought he was walking through a tropical jungle. This advanced stage of hypothermia is called paradoxical disrobing. Victims in this severely confused state often experience hallucinations of warmth, just before slipping into a coma and then dying. Many of the fortunate few who have survived severe hypothermia recount similar tricks of the brain that seemed all too real at the time.

Whole books are written about hypothermia. It is the number-one killer in survival mishaps. It used to be called "death by exposure," a term still seen in some headlines today. The primary purpose of a shelter is to help the body maintain its proper level of body heat by regulating itself if too cold or too hot. Since about 70 to 80°F (21 to 27°C) is the ideal surrounding temperature in which most humans can operate with no loss or gain in body core temperature, any environment beyond those narrow limits will affect the body's effort to regulate itself. Too warm and the body starts actions that cool down; too cold and those functions reverse to initiate a warming process.

Most humans have an internal body temperature within about three degrees of the average 98.6°F (37°C). The body's temperature will normally vary three or four degrees beyond that range with everyday activity. It's when we push our body beyond those limits and beyond its natural ability to regulate our temperature that we have to augment that internal system through external means of warming or cooling. Failing to maintain those adjust-ments is what gets a person into trouble. Lose too much heat and hypothermia sets in. Failure to cool sufficiently often results in hyperthermia.

The clothes we wear and the shelters we build to protect

us play a critical role in our ability to maintain those regulated temperatures during a survival situation. Proper clothing means clothing designed to perform in a certain way under certain conditions. It should keep you warm, or cool, and should keep you dry no matter what climatic conditions surround you. To do so it should fit properly (not too tight) and comfortably.

Our bodies produce warmth in two ways:

➤ We create it internally by processing fuel (food) and by working our muscles; heat is gained through metabolism or the burning of calories.

➤ We gain it externally from absorption (radiated from the sun) or from other sources.

We lose heat in five ways:

➤ **Radiation:** heat loss from exposed areas of skin.

➤ **Conduction:** a transfer of heat from our body to any colder surface (the main cause of body heat loss).

➤ **Respiration:** heat lost from warming inhaled cold air and then exhaling that air.

➤ **Evaporation:** heat lost as the body turns moisture into vapor.

➤ **Convection:** heat lost by transfer through air or liquid.

Clothing, properly worn in layers, can help your body's temperature-regulating mechanisms function properly to best perform their warming, or cooling, tasks.

As a Scout, one of the first ways I learned to be prepared was to make a list of clothing I would need on an outing. Knowing where we were going helped me determine the type of clothing I should bring. That decision was based on the anticipated activities, weather and terrain. Even today as I prepare for an afternoon or extended stay, I use the same system. I start at my feet and work my way to the top of my head, determining each article of clothing as I go.

Footgear

Our heart may be the engine, our stomach the fuel tank, but our feet are clearly the wheels of the human vehicle. What we select for our "tires" is very important.

Shoes or boots must fit properly. Don't assume your street size is your hiking size. Thick stockings and swollen feet may mean a larger size is needed than what you buy for your casual shoe. Fit your boots carefully. It is also very important to break in shoes and boots gradually, certainly before wearing them for an extended period of time or distance.

Footwear should be well insulated. It must offer support to the ankles and arches. Good footgear will protect your entire foot from toe to ankle and a bit beyond. In addition, it must provide proper and secure traction for the type of terrain being traversed. Most boots should be waterproof, while others, such as jungle boots, are designed to get wet but then drain and dry fast. Some boots are extremely flexible, while others are actually two boots: an inner liner and a hard outer shell (similar to a ski boot).

Cold-weather boots may include either a sewn-in liner or come with a separate, insulated booty (usually made of felt or a quilted material). Care of your feet and boots means drying both when you can. The nice feature about the removable bootie is that it can be pulled from the outer shell, thus ensuring that both have a better chance at drying adequately.

Many hiking boots and shoes are specifically designed for certain use—casual walking, multiple-terrain hiking, rock scrambling and so on. Tough synthetic materials, in both the soles and side/top panels, make these boots rugged (usually not as tough as leather, however) and much lighter. Most are laced; some feature innovative latches and clips for securing the boot to the wearer's foot. Remember the concept of multiple use? Those shoe laces are very handy when you need cord to lash a shelter, tie a signal cloth to a pole or hold a bandage compress over a wound.

Makeshift footwear can be fabricated from a variety of materials, natural and man-made. In a survival situation you can fashion sandals from large slabs of bark, foldover foot coverings from car mats or carpet pieces, or fabricate classic Neanderthal footwear from pieces of animal hide wrapped and tied to your feet—all can be created to protect one's feet.

The most basic footgear has been worn to accomplish some amazing feats. The first successful ascent to the summit of Alaska's Denali (also known as Mount McKinley), the tallest peak in North America, was made by a group of adventurers led by an Alaskan Native named Walter Harper. He climbed to the top of that 20,320-foot (6,197-m) peak wearing thick, moose-hide moccasins and several layers of wool socks.

Socks
The effectiveness of the best boot is severely diminished

without a good sock or two between the bare foot and the boot. Typically socks are made from natural fibers such as wool or cotton or various synthetic materials such as nylon or polyester. A thin, lightweight stocking works as a good first layer, wicking moisture away from the foot and reducing friction, which 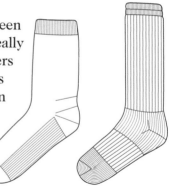 prevents blisters from forming. A second, thicker layer of wool or synthetic adds insulation as it cushions the foot and protects against cold weather. Regardless of all the modern materials, I doubt there is anything truly better than a thick pair of wool stockings inside a good pair of leather boots.

Survival Tip: Water Filter

Socks are very versatile survival tools. Stuffing grasses, clean sand, charcoal and other straining materials into a sock transforms it into a crude, but effective, water filter.

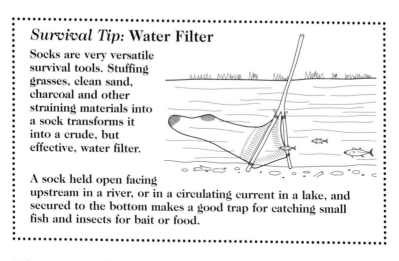

A sock held open facing upstream in a river, or in a circulating current in a lake, and secured to the bottom makes a good trap for catching small fish and insects for bait or food.

Whatever you find that works for you, make sure your feet are kept dry with good circulation from a proper-fitting and laced boot and by having extra socks along. In an emergency situation, wearing a few thick layers of wool stockings without boots may be your best bet. Remember that natural insulators such as grass, cattails and milkweed can be stuffed into your socks for added warmth around camp and while sleeping.

Gaiters

I can't forget to put a plug in for gaiters, those lower leggings that strap around your instep and cover your leg from ankle to calf. Gaiters help keep your boots and lower pants legs drier. Some are nothing more than a tie-string and an inexpensive nylon sleeve. Others are made of breathable fabric and strategically reinforced with webbing. I use mine while snowshoeing or hiking in the early morning while the dew clings to the tall meadow grasses.

First Layer

Underwear, the layer of clothing next to your skin, is a very important layer. It must wick body perspiration and moisture away from your skin. It should be soft and smooth so it doesn't irritate your skin. It should be easy to clean. Dirty clothing does not function as it should when spaces between the weave clog and render many fabrics much less useful.

Survival Tip: **Makeshift Compass**

It is sometimes possible to use silk to create a makeshift compass. Stroke a small needle or thin razor blade several times in one direction with a piece of silk to line up the charges in that metal to form a magnet. It's a weak "charge" but when the needle or blade is suspended from a thin thread, it will swing to magnetic north.

In maritime environments or colder climates, a saying most everyone swears by is "Cotton kills!" When wet, cotton is heavy, has no insulating value and is said to draw away warmth 25 times faster than air. Cotton does not wick water; it absorbs it. However, cotton is often the fabric of choice in drier, hotter climates. One type of cotton undergarment popular in Scandinavian countries, the "fishnet" undershirt, wicks away moisture and actually creates a layer of air pockets in the spaces between the strands of netting.

Here is a list of some fabrics used in outdoor garments, with pros and cons of usage:

➤ **Cotton** should be considered a warm- or hot-weather fabric, as wet cotton is useless, absorbs water and robs the body of warmth.

➤ **Wool** retains its insulating quality when wet and can be a real lifesaver. However, it is heavy and doesn't compact well. It can also be very itchy.

➤ **Polypropylene** is extremely warm, does not absorb moisture and is notorious for retaining body odors that require a good washing to rid. I have a pair of poly long johns that are so warm I rarely wear them in the winter. Instead I pack them for emergency use.

➤ **Polyester** easily challenges wool as the best all-around fabric. It's a good insulator, warms fairly well even when wet and tends to absorb little water. It also compacts nicely. Most "fleece" clothing is made from polyester. If it gets wet, wring it out and put it back on—great for maritime environments.

➤ **Nylon** comes in various weaves and is a popular fabric for making outer shells. Some are waterproof, while others are woven to be more breathable. Nylon compacts well and, depending upon the original size of the article, can be stuffed into incredibly small spaces.

You will never see pilots and aircrews wearing synthetic materials. Those fabrics will melt and fuse to the body when exposed to high temperatures or flames. Most natural materials, on the other hand, will just burn when exposed to flames.

Second Layer

This should be a loose-fitting layer that protects your neck, arms and wrists. This is a transitional layer; it serves as an outer, removable garment in temperate or hot climates or a middle layer in cooler conditions. This layer can be constructed using a variety of materials as well. It should be worn to wick the moisture away from the underlayer, transferring it either to the third (outer) layer or by directing moisture out through the neck and wrist openings. This layer should also have insulating qualities to help retain body heat.

In situations where you do not have sufficient insulation, get out of the wind or other elements and use those natural insulating materials discussed earlier (cattails, grass, etc.) to stuff inside this layer. Pulling your arms in next to your torso can retain extra warmth.

Third Layer

This layer can be either the outer layer in fluctuating milder climates or a middle layer between the wicking core and the protective outer shell in colder environments. It's the layer that should be monitored closely, as it absorbs the moisture/perspiration from the inner layer. In cold climates it's often the layer that is peeled off and changed whenever the wearer becomes too hot or damp. At that point the outer shell may need to be vented to help regulate excess heat and moisture transfer.

Most often this layer is made of fleece, pile or wool. A drawback with fleece and pile as outer layers is that they usually don't block the wind, although some new fabrics do offer some protection from penetrating airflow.

Outermost Layer

This is the layer exposed to the elements; it's your shelter—the shelter you wear. In hot/sunny environments it provides shade. In cold climates it insulates against low temperatures and chilling winds. It's also your rain shelter as needed. This outer layer should either "breathe" (allow moisture to escape but not enter) or have ways to easily vent without compromising the integrity of the shell (adjustable hoods, underarm vents, etc.). One note of caution: You do not want your outer layer flapping in the breeze if you are trying to maintain a certain level of warmth. Too much airflow under this outer shell will disperse too much heat.

Survival Tip: **Clothing Uses**

Outer garments can contain a treasure trove of survival items.

➤ The drawstrings on your parka or jacket hood are cordage for myriad uses.

➤ The hood could be removed to make a temporary sock or boot liner.

➤ The zipper pull can be fashioned into a fishing lure.

➤ A brightly colored, outer garment can be waved as an emergency signal.

➤ A waterproof raincoat can be used to create a basin for collecting water off a tent fly or can be a collecting surface of its own to direct rainwater into another container.

➤ Lint collected along the edges of seams or deep in pocket corners can be used as tinder for starting fires.

Also, wider seams can be opened and emergency items (lighters, extra knife, etc.) can be sewn in for handy access in the event of an emergency.

My experience with "breathable" fabric is that its effectiveness depends upon the rate of perspiration produced by an individual. Profuse sweating exceeds the transfer of moisture rate of most breathable materials, creating excess moisture under the shell. This overload requires venting or some other way of getting rid of the excess moisture. It can be a real tug-of-war when rain forces you to seal up your "breathable" rain gear while your body is kicking out copious amounts of perspiration because you are so hot. Eventually the body will regulate itself and regain a balance, but excess moisture becomes a threat as it builds up in your core layer. This may be the time to change one or two of those inner layers.

The most common outer layer for winter activity is the insulated parka. I find 3M's Thinsulate among the best insulating materials in clothing where I do not want a lot of bulk. I've been fortunate with goose down for extremely low temperatures. Synthetic materials are often preferred over down for the simple reason that wet down is worthless. In a cold environment, it's possibly a killer. DuPont's family of Polarguard fills are among the popular insulating materials used today.

Another excellent material that I highly recommend is Lamilite insulation used by Wiggy's, Inc. It's an unbonded, silicone-treated, continuous filament fiber that does not require quilting or tube construction. It is also incredibly compactible yet returns to nearly all of its initial loft.

Pants
The advantages of each material discussed earlier apply to pants and leggings as well. The inner layer is usually covered by a heavier middle layer that, in turn, is covered by an outer shell. Thick, durable cotton is popular as a rugged, all-purpose fabric, especially where it will experience a lot of abuse. Again, wet cotton is heavy and provides no insulation.

In some climates, chaps or other leggings are worn over

cotton pants. As long as the cotton stays dry, these are good combinations. Insulated bibs and breathable outer pants shells are also popular and effective. Rugged nylon pants are also quite popular and come in a variety of styles.

Head Gear

More than 25 percent of your body heat is lost through your exposed head! It follows then, to conserve more heat, cover your head. Conversely, to vent excess heat, uncover it. A wide-brimmed hat provides shade and keeps the rain out of the wearer's eyes or off glasses. Some hats have a neck flap that shades the back of the neck from sun. It also protects against drafts. A cotton hat can be soaked in water to effectively become a mini air conditioner to help cool you off through evaporation. Some hats have small vents along their base to let warm air escape.

A satisfactory head covering is a bandana. It'll keep sweat out of your eyes, and when dampened, will cool your head. Any Boy Scout should be familiar with other uses of the bandana, from all the training with the Scout neckerchief. Besides being part of the official dress uniform, the neckerchief serves well as a triangular bandage, arm sling and sprained ankle support in first aid applications. Don't forget to get a few bandanas in bright colors—they make good signal flags.

Survival Tip: **Feet Warmer**

If your feet are cold, cover your head with a cap or hat. You'll feel the tingle of warm toes in a matter of minutes.

Hand Gear

One of my warmest hand coverings is a pair of classic leather "chopper" mittens with a rough, scratchy wool liner mitt. I keep a spare pair in my car. I have graduated to expedition-grade down mittens for those really cold days, and I also have a pair of waterproof, Thinsulate-lined gloves with long gauntlet-like extensions into which I can tuck the sleeves of my outer jacket.

At the beginning of the cold season I usually wear a thin poly glove liner inside my mitten or glove until my hands acclimate to where I can go gloveless for extended periods of time. As a safety precaution, however, I have pairs of such liner gloves stuffed into several pockets in my jackets and backpacks.

The fabrics listed earlier, with the same attributes, benefits and limitations are also used in constructing gloves and mittens. Like all other clothing, hand gear should fit well and keep you dry. Liners alone or just the outer shells can be used in emergency situations for keeping hands warm. A little extra insulation can be added to mittens using the cattail/milkweed/grass filler discussed earlier. This last trick works for small children; it'll work for you: Tie each end of a cord around each cuff on your mittens run the cord up inside one sleeve and down the other so you can remove your gloves or mittens without losing them.

EQUIPMENT BAG

Carrying gear in the field is made quite easy today, thanks to the myriad styles of daypacks, backpacks and fanny/belt packs in the marketplace. While some companies still produce packs made from rugged canvas, most are made from strong nylons, such as ripstop or Cordura. Awkward and bulky external-frame packs of yesteryear (near right) have almost totally been replaced with internal-frame packs

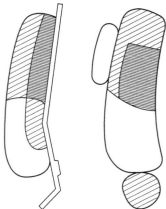

(far right) that are ergonomically designed to better conform to the wearer's torso.

Each company designs its bags with various styles and quantities of pockets, zippered closures and removable compartments. Features vary, so personal need and degree of utility are key factors in deciding which type of pack will work best for you. Some packs are merely large, one-compartment bags for carrying an assortment of gear a short distance, such as the legendary Duluth Pack made popular by voyageurs for use on long canoe portages. At the other end of the spectrum are the fanny/belt packs worn by joggers and casual hikers to store film sunglasses or other small personal items.

Whatever you choose, make sure seams are strong and multi-stitched. Zippers and strap connections should be strong and durable, too. Waterproof pockets or liners are valuable extras sometimes offered. Some packs break away into smaller pouches and mini-packs. Consider such options to store and carry your first aid and survival kit. Remember, if it's not on you—carried with you—you won't have it when you need it.

SLEEPING BAG

In the upper ranks of important survival gear are the sleeping bag and its cousin, the bivy sack. Sleeping bags probably evolved from the classic bedroll used by travelers for thousands of years consisting of a few blankets and perhaps a ground cloth. Most modern sleeping bags appear similar in design, construction and materials. How-ever, a closer inspection and knowing what to look for can make the differences much more apparent.

Shape

There used to be just two shapes of bags: the classic

military "mummy" bag (near right) with its characteristic hood, and the traditional, plaid-flannel-lined rectangular sleeping bag. Mummy bags are filled with down (goose or duck) and quite compactible. Rectangular 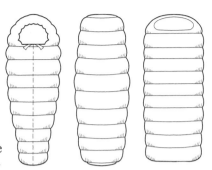 bags (middle) are filled with several kinds of insulating materials and are rather bulky.

Today, a third shape is available (far right). These hybrid bags combine the features of both bags, offering the hood of the mummy and the more square body and boxed foot area of the rectangular models. Sleeping bag designers also have recently discovered that women are built differently than men and are now offering sleeping bags proportionally shaped to better serve the female body. New "sleeping systems" (as bags are referred to these days) are also designed with more shoulder room (no more of that straight-jacket tightness) and expandable body panels to add girth and, thus, more volume to the bag. Other features to make the bags more efficient at retaining heat and maintaining comfort are being added at every opportunity.

Temperature Rating
Sleeping bags are categorized by their temperature range and seasonal use. A three-season bag is generally the standard bag for everything but extreme winter camping. The temperature rating for these bags may range between 20°F and 40°F (–6°C and 4°C). This is an arbitrary range that suggests the comfort level for an average person. A four-season bag would be the choice for most winter camping. It is best to determine the range of temperatures

in which you expect to use your bag and then go down about several degrees more just to be safe.

There are summer bags, generally called "ultra-lights," that are for taking the chill off of cool summer evenings. At the other end of the temperature scale, there are extreme cold-weather expedition bags that will keep a person warm at −20°F, −30°F, even −40°F (−29°C, −34°C, −40°C).

Insulation Materials

The key to a sleeping bag's effectiveness is, of course, the type of insulation used and, to a lesser but still important degree, the construction methods used to secure that insulation in place. Like clothing, there are two types of insulation materials used in sleeping bags: natural and synthetic fibers.

➤ **Natural:** Down is the gold standard of insulation. It provides the most warmth for the least weight. It's usually the most expensive fill and does carry the down "curse"—it's useless when wet! The highest quality of down is the underlayer feathers from geese. Cheaper down comes from ducks. Warmth is often determined by "loft." The loftiness of the down is referenced by a number (e.g. 500 down, 700 down). This refers to the number of cubic inches (cm) of space that 1 ounce (28 g) of that particular down will occupy. The bigger the number, the loftier the down. More loft equals more warmth.

➤ **Synthetic:** Imagine long, continuous, minute-diameter fibers (some are even hollow) winding endlessly throughout a sleeping bag to form an insulation layer consisting of thousands of tiny air spaces between each fiber (and within that hollow core). That's the essence of the newer synthetic fibers such as the Polarguard family of materials from DuPont. They all approach down in loft and insulating characteristics. They do exceed down in one key area: They still perform when wet (unlike down, synthetics do not retain moisture).

Most synthetic materials don't compress as well as down and are notably heavier. Generally, synthetic bags are less expensive than down for the same temperature range. Synthetic bags are easier to clean but don't tend to last as long as down.

Some manufacturers have developed their own specialized synthetic insulation and treat it to perform in certain, proprietary ways. Some companies even combine down and synthetic fibers to try to offer the best of both worlds.

Construction
Most bags use several different structural ways to align and secure their filling. The filling may be confined in a tube or contained within the quilted pattern or some other means that forms an insulating shell around the bag. How these seams are joined and whether or not the insulation overlaps at those seams (where the tubes come together or at each border of the quilting pattern) can determine whether or not the bag will have any "cold spots," a result of a thin layer of insulation at those seams. The warmest bag I have allows the insulation to conform around me, minimizing the amount of air space being heated by my body.

The outer shell of a sleeping bag is important, as it must be rugged, help contain your body heat and protect you from the elements. Shell material comes with a variety of different labels. Some tend to be more water resistant than others while some claim to be highly breathable. They are all designed to help keep out wind and rain. Most are made of synthetic fibers such as nylon or polyester. Very inexpensive bags are still made with cotton outer shells. These are best used in a protected environment such as a cabin or camper unit only. They rarely perform well when exposed to the elements.

Other important features in a modern sleeping bag include a draft tube to keep the wind from nipping its way into the bag along the zipper. Some bags feature a draft collar (either insulated or made of special fabric such as fleece) to keep drafts from entering around your neck.

All sleeping bags come with stuff sacks. If yours is brightly colored, there's one more signaling device.

BIVY SACK

These usually come in two styles: those that form an outer shell slightly bigger than a sleeping bag and those that are a cross between a sleeping shell and a body poncho. The first style performs as a mini tent. They are usually quick to pitch and provide a very confined, sheltered air space in which to sleep.

Some bivy sacks have a drawstring around the waist and two arm slits so the wearer can sit up and perform basic tasks while still fully protected inside a sack that doubles as a sleeping bag. Outer shells of bivy sacks are typically made of ripstop nylon or various weights of Cordura nylon.

PONCHO

These are a great multiple-use piece of gear serving not only as loose-fitting rain gear, but also as a ground cloth, a lean-to roof and, if brightly colored, a signal. Some ponchos are strong enough to be used as the covering of a makeshift litter for transporting victims.

I recently found a new piece of outdoor equipment that is two distinct pieces of gear literally rolled—or folded—into one. Designed by Stephen Yardan, the DeltaShelter is worn zipped and folded as a poncho. When unfolded and unzipped, it is a completely functional one-person dome tent. This versatile, self-contained unit can be used as an emergency shelter on the trail or provide an extra, quick shelter in base camp for someone who needs to be kept warm and dry.

When refolded and worn as a poncho, its hardware (tent poles, stakes) is neatly stored within the poncho. It's as though MacGyver and Professor Gadget joined forces to produce an innovative piece of survival gear. It is an ingenious product, marketed by Stearns Inc.

SLEEPING PAD

These provide both an insulating and cushioning layer between your sleeping bag and the ground. There are basically two types of pads: those that self-inflate and allow you to adjust firmness by the use of an air valve, and those that are closed-cell foam and come in various thicknesses and degrees of firmness. Of course the main disadvantage of the self-inflating type is that it can be punctured and, although rarely, it can rupture. Repairs are easily made with duct tape or silicone-based glues or "goos."

These pads and their smaller kin sold as pillows and other comfort pads can also be used as makeshift splints, cervical collars or emergency footwear. Such pads are valuable around camp, too, as comfy seat cushions or as a base to stand on while changing clothes.

TENT

The tent is our house in the woods. It's our protection against most elements. It's a place for congregating, a storage area for our belongings and the roof under which we sleep. A tent needs to be a moderately secure structure—both rainproof and windproof. Typically, most survival situations occur without such a basic luxury being available; hence, the importance of learning the skills necessary to improvise a shelter.

Tents have evolved as fabric replicas of traditional shelters used by nomadic humans for thousands of years. The yurt structure from Asia, the Navajo "hogan" from America's Southwest, even the pioneer's cabin have been recreated in tent shapes. The tipi of the American Plains Indian continues to be the tent shape of choice for some.

Recent innovations make it possible to have a tent that literally pitches itself (through the use of inflatable air tubes instead of tent poles, for example).

A good tent is lightweight yet durable. It is usually ventilated with window-like panels covered in small mesh insect netting. (While most tents offer insect screening, make sure the mesh is small enough to prevent very small flies, called "no-see-ums," from penetrating the screen.) Secured tent flaps are sealed with sturdy zippers. A "tub" or "bath" floor (the floor fabric that extends up each side of the tent for several inches/cm) helps prevent moisture from creeping up from the bottom of the tent.

Most tents that utilize a tent fly, a separate outer shell that is waterproof, have an inner roof that is either netting or some other breathable material. Dome and tunnel tents all use an external pole framework from which to hang the tent shell. The tent fly is spread over this framework, providing both the water-proof roof and a sunscreen for the tent.

Both tents and flies should have a good system of guy lines for securing to the ground. A variety of stakes are available for different ground conditions, from loose sand to hardpacked clay—even stakes for use in snow country. You don't want to have to go out in foul weather to re-secure your tent—make sure it's properly staked and secure the first time.

The tent provides the security of a shelter and helps a person stay fairly comfortable and rested—all good conditions for nurturing a positive attitude and alertness. Make sure you've selected a tent site that is not in danger from its surroundings, such as overhead limbs, falling branches, high tides or seasonal drainage.

As a Boy Scout I was taught to "ditch" my tent. Not throw it away, but dig a small trench or ditch completely around the base of the tent. Any water running off the tent roof was channeled away from the tent once it reached the ground. Today, of course, this is an environmental no-no. There could be, however, an extreme case where torrents of ground water could warrant digging a network of ditches to guide water away from your tent. It would be better to anticipate such a possibility and pitch your tent to avoid that situation.

HAMMOCK
Hammocks have always been an alternative option for sleeping—the idyllic repose, swinging between two palm trees at the edge of a tropical sea. Several companies offer hammocks with a weatherproof roof and insect screening similar to a tent. In fact, such hammocks could be described as hanging tents. There are, of course, pros and cons to the use of a hammock.

The pro side lists the ease of pitching, no need to worry about ground conditions (rocky, swamp, too uneven) on which to securely or comfortably pitch a tent and the shear comfort of being gracefully cradled in the hammock's sling.

Drawbacks include limited space for gear and little practical "living" space, an uninsulated floor (some manufacturers are addressing this issue with pad inserts and other innovations) and the limited back support.

KNIFE
The second most vital survival tool after a positive mental attitude is a knife! By cutting, scraping, poking, drilling and chopping, it is the one tool that can help you acquire all your other vital survival gear. It can be used to make a wide assortment of other tools, can facilitate devising a shelter, help fabricate emergency clothing and make it easier to harvest or forage for edible plants or animals.

There are many knife configurations from which

to choose. Blades come in a variety of lengths, grades of steel, shapes and uses. There are knives with fixed blades, with blades that fold into a handle and even a knife that has two blades that revolve around a central pivoting pin. There are knives with uninterrupted straight edges, multiple serrated edges and some with sharpened, hooked blades. There are some with more tools blossoming from their main housing or handle than the entire hardware section at Sears.

The classic bowie knife is a rather large example of a fixed-blade knife. The blade tang extends back into the handle providing for one-piece construction and structural integrity throughout the knife. It's going to take a mighty severe force to break the blade. Fixed-blade knives can be used to cut some pretty formidable branches, either by shear cutting power or with added striking force on the back edge of the blade to drive it through larger branches.

There are some very high quality folding knives on the market today. Some can be opened with the quick flick of the thumb. Several companies make pocket knife kits that are a tool chest of accessories. The biggest problem with a folding knife is the pin on which the blade pivots. Too much pressure on such blades can cause the pin to snap or the blade to fail at that point.

It's important to know how to sharpen a knife and know how to use it—the right knife for the right job. A sharp knife is a safe knife. A well-sharpened blade bites rather than slips and can usually be controlled better. So no matter what type of knife you choose, make sure it will sharpen up to a useable edge. Blades are typically made from either carbon steel or stainless steel. Carbon steel is softer, so it sharpens easier than stainless. Within each of those options are various grades of steel. Before you buy a knife, take some time to learn these differences.

In a survival mode without a knife, think of the basic form and function of that tool: a sharpened edge for cutting and a safe way to grip the blade. With that in mind, a thin strip of metal, a shard of glass, chipped pottery, even some seashells can be formed into serviceable cutting edges. An advantage with glass and some rocks is that you can chip or break off a new edge once the present edge becomes worn and dull. You can also use some fine, but hard-grained, flat rocks to keep a useable edge on most knives.

Hatchets can be vital tools as well. Heavier than most knives, a hatchet is perhaps left behind because of its weight. However, there are a few good "survival" hatchets available that are compact, can keep a knife-sharp edge and can be used in a variety of ways.

Survival Tip: **Makeshift Mirror**
The shiny side of either a knife or hatchet blade can be used as a reflector mirror for signaling.

MULTI-USE EQUIPMENT

I'll discuss specific items in future chapters that relate directly to certain tools and materials. The most important thing to remember is the concept of multiple-use capabilities of tools. The more tasks you can complete with the same tool, the more options you have at your disposal. For instance, can that piece of gear also hold water? Can it be used as a signaling device? Could you use it to make a signal? If you take a tool down to its basics, you can more easily improvise. For example, you may not have a shovel, but you do have a pan lid. Even a pointed stick can be used to break up and loosen soil so you can dig with your fingers.

Think of the versatile garbage bag! It serves its primary purpose as a container for trash or gear. It's also a makeshift raincoat, shelter roofing material, emergency clothing, signaling device, cordage made from woven strips, ground cloth, wash basin. If you think about it, there are sure to be more uses.

A positive mental attitude, coupled with a basic under-standing of survival techniques and some common sense, will help you come up with some very creative alternative uses for the tools at hand.

Chapter 4

The Importance of Shelter

A weekend caribou hunting trip began as planned for an Alaskan pilot and his twelve-year-old son. Upon taking off from a remote lake 200 miles (320 km) from Anchorage, their PA-18 Super Cub on floats suddenly flipped over on take-off and became stuck in the muddy bottom of the shallow lake. September temperatures were in the 50s (10 to 15°C); winds were 10 to 15 mph (16 to 24 kmph), gusting higher at times until reaching about 40 knots by nightfall. The surrounding landscape was typical caribou country—flat open country, covered in tundra-like vegetation with no trees.

The two stranded hunters were wearing standard dress for Alaskan bush flying— inflatable CO_2 survival vests, synthetic clothing and hip boots. Father and son managed to make it to shore after crawling out of the inverted plane. They were able to salvage a small amount of gear floating in the water. The father had to cut a hole into the fuselage of the plane and push as much gear as he could toward the opening to remove it from the plane. Unable to extract their tent, they retrieved two sleeping bags. After a half hour of recovering gear, the wet pair managed to get what they could of their completely drenched equipment to shore.

Realizing that he and his son were both showing early signs of hypothermia, the pilot sought refuge behind a small bush that blocked some of the wind. The ground was soggy and wet with no trees or usable firewood within sight. The father had considered trying to reach higher ground, but the winds would have been worse. The two stripped off much of their wet clothing and sought the protection of the limited space of the father's larger sleeping bag.

Covering themselves with the other sleeping bag (both of which were soaking wet when retrieved from the plane), the father began warming enough to start taking other survival measures. He was able to find a cook stove and meager provisions as the salvaged gear washed up on the shore of the lake. He also found extra batteries in his life vest that enabled him to use his satellite phone. He and his son enjoyed a cup of hot cocoa as he phoned for help. As he made his life-saving call he noticed that the bags, in addition to being warm even though they had been soaked, were now starting to dry out in the wind. Their wet clothing was splayed out on nearby branches for the wind to dry, and the two crash victims sat back and waited.

Fortunately, they had prepared a plan ahead of time. The pilot had left their hunting area navigational coordinates with his wife. A state trooper pilot was able to fly directly to their crash site and rescue them before nightfall, when temperatures would have dropped to the lower 20s (below 0°C).

So many survival scenarios share these same factors: a sudden and unexpected incident that immediately places a person or party into a life-threatening survival situation. In this case, preparations ahead of time, the importance of a shelter, quality gear selection, and skills and experience saved lives.

WHERE TO BUILD

Shelters can be either natural or man-made. Chapter 3 discussed man-made tents and other fabric shelters. We've also discussed how clothing is the most intimate shelter, the one you wear on your back. Sometimes your clothing and a small space beneath a clump of vegetation may be the only shelter you can find. The importance of good clothing is ever present. And don't forget that roof you can wear on your head— a good hat!

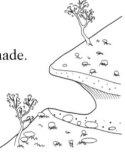

Natural shelters can be found or built. Part of the initial assessment of an area, once injuries are noted and treated, is the inventory for materials and locations for a shelter.

In most temperate climates, shelters can be constructed using a variety of foliage and trees in the area. Shelters must be secure from imposing dangers such as falling rocks, tree limbs, unblocked winds, exposure to the elements and so on. Knowing how to read an area will help you select a proper shelter site.

➤ Does the ground appear to collect and hold water after
  a rain?

➤ Are the limbs on trees windswept in a particular
  direction?

➤ Are there any other signs that indicate unfriendly
  natural forces affecting the area?

Your location should be visible from the air, if possible, or
in an area that typically might be checked by search and
rescue teams—near water, for example. Creating a shelter
too deep within the forest, away from a clearing, can make
your camp unseen from the air. Since staying in one
location is a key factor in being rescued, picking a safe
shelter and creating good signals—visible from the air or
great distances—tie together when selecting a site. However, do not place your camp in major animal thorough-
fares, especially along trails frequented by bears. In fact,
all food preparation should be made away from your
campsite.

Another consideration in
site selection is the number
of people in your party and
the extent of resources
available. There may be
limited food and water
supplies and even limited
materials for everyone to
make an adequate shelter.

Site hygiene is important, too. Though probably limited,
refuse and human waste may build to a point that diging a
latrine or moving to a new location may become
necessary.

The terrain and season will affect your shelter location.

For example:

➤ Desert country will suggest natural shaded areas, if possible, and proximity to a water source.

➤ Snow country offers a variety of shelter options—snow caves, igloo-type structures, even snow trenches—but take care to avoid avalanches, collapsing overhangs of snow (cornices, excessive snow on tree branches) and extensive drifting.

➤ In hilly or canyon country be aware of warming eastern and southern slopes and that cool air flows down a canyon at night. Stay on the east or south slopes or higher up for the warmest sites.

WHEN TO BUILD

A key element in prioritizing your survival plan is deciding when to build a shelter. Ask the average outdoors person what he or she would do first, and most will say, "Light a fire." The following scenario explains why building a fire first is not usually a good plan.

Imagine you and a couple of friends are out on an afternoon hiking trip and become hopelessly lost. It's nearing dusk and the decision is made to stay put for the night and make a plan of action the next morning. Since you had not prepared for this delay, you have very limited food and no equipment for the extended stay (tent, sleeping bags, etc.). You collectively decide to build a fire. You all gather firewood and attempt to start a fire. The only book of matches among you turns out to be soggy from perspiration, so one member attempts to start a fire with a magnesium/striker kit recently purchased but never used.

Nearly an hour after deciding to make camp, the group is

tired and frustrated at having failed to start a fire. While concentrat-ing on that task, the weather worsened, and it begins to rain. Within a few minutes the group that had been dry and toasty warm is now soaked from head to toe. The rain quits, the winds pick up and the tempera-ture drops. You have no shelter. You spent all your dry time trying to start a fire. If you had started a shelter first, you would probably be dry—or drier—and could attempt starting your fire in a more comfortable state. Now you must frantically build a shelter as hypothermia—always a danger—is now a much more imminent threat.

Don't dismiss the alternatives, however. If there are enough people in your group, perhaps a few can start working on a fire while a few others gather materials and start making a shelter. You may also be in a situation where a fire will be necessary to treat a victim of advanc-ing hypothermia. It could also be prudent to start a fire for signaling if you are reasonably sure it would be seen by a passerby (a scheduled ferry run along a coastline, for example). The key here, as in all survival situations, is to make a wise choice based on preparation, prior knowledge and your best gut feelings. In the long run, it is usually better to make a shelter, even a temporary one, before starting fires or undertaking other tasks.

WHAT TO BUILD
Your location and the season will play big parts in deter-mining the kind of shelter you build. Some types will work almost anywhere; some are only viable in particular situations.

Go "Undercover"
Often the simplest shelter is a small depression or enclos-ure created by branches or limbs of a tree or large bush. Protection from the wind, rain and low temperatures are your primary concerns.

I am more than 6½ feet (2 m) tall, and I once created a rather comfortable temporary shelter under a log just above the high water mark on a beach in Alaska. The 18-inch-diameter (45.7-cm) log had been washed up onto its position by a past winter storm and subsequent winds and rain had hollowed out an opening underneath the log. I filled in the backside with beach sand and a few scavenged boards (which I first used as makeshift shovels to clear more sand away from under the log).

I then completely stuffed the cavity under the log with beach grass I harvested from the surrounding area. I burrowed and squirmed down into this grassy nest and pulled layers of matted grass up around me. I was protected from the wind and most rain assaults and was adequately insulated from the drop in temperature typical for the season.

A simple and practical winter shelter is the space commonly found at the base of evergreen trees in snow country. This is typically a space beneath the lower, snow-laden branches that droop nearly to the ground. The space around the trunk of the tree is usually big enough to at least squat under. Stuffing dry grasses into that space can add needed insulation.

Survival Tip: **Shelter Vent**

Any enclosed space, either natural or man-made, may need to be vented, especially if a fire is built inside the shelter, to allow carbon dioxide to escape.

Lean-to

When I was a kid, there wasn't a summer that went by when we didn't build a "fort" in the woods. The earliest versions of our lean-tos evolved into more sophisticated designs as we learned from our Boy Scout training how to

lash poles together and create more
solid structures. Little did we know
that we were learning a skill that
could become a life-saving task.

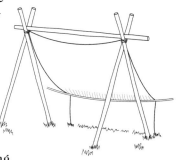

The lean-to is probably the most
common structure constructed
in emergency situations.
Whether it is an open-sided
shelter with a pitched roof extending
to the ground or a center ridgepole leaning against the
fork of a tree, the principles of construction are the same.
A lean-to is simply a horizontal or inclined support pole
to which branches and other roofing/siding materials are
added to create a one-sided, sloped-roof, windproof,
rainproof shelter. The lean-to should be tall enough for a
person to sit up as well as lie down comfortably. The roof
is made by first framing a lattice network of supporting
branches or twigs. More leafed branches are then added.
A layer of roofing is built up and secured so rain will not
readily penetrate the shelter. Flooring and addition
insulation made from grasses and natural materials can
then be added.

A common lean-to method is using a rain poncho as the
roof, secured to a supporting cross branch lashed between
two trees.

Snow Shelter
In addition to natural shelters often formed in winter,
such as at the base of trees, you may need to construct a
shelter in the cold. It can be as simple as piling up snow,
making a snow dome, and then carving out a space inside.

An igloo-shaped shelter can be created by first stacking
several packs (or other bulky, basic-shaped items)
together and then piling snow on top of this heap to

create a mound of snow. As you add layers of snow to the pile, pause between each layer to allow the snow to settle and even begin evaporating. As the ice crystals in the snow change form they lock together forming a tighter bond. This, in turn, creates a firmer structure.

Once the pile of snow seems big enough for two people to crawl into, carefully start digging away an entrance-sized opening inward from the base of the mound. You should reach your packs and be able to pull them free and out of the pile. This creates an oddly shaped but hollow center to the mound. You can carefully scrape away more snow inside to smooth off and expand the inner walls. Insulate the floor of the shelter with reeds, grasses and leaves.

Last, but very important, is to make a ledge or shelf above the floor in a snow shelter so your body is above where cold air settles. If you are in a snow cave or dome, pull a backpack or other "plug" behind you and wedge it into the entrance for a makeshift door.

The most basic winter shelter in flat country may be a
shallow trench, lined with a thick layer of natural insulation and covered with either branches or slabs of snow
broken or cut from a crusty top layer.

When creating a snow shelter, whether it's a mound of
snow or a snow cave (cut into the side of a solid snow wall
or snow mass) it is important to keep the size of the
shelter small. Never make a shelter bigger than that which
will effectively provide room for three inhabitants. In cold
weather, a vital survival exercise is to sleep three abreast,
alternating in and out of the middle position to gain extra
body warmth from the two outside bodies.

Desert Shelter

Keeping cool and hydrated, and avoiding heat stroke and
sunburn are the biggest concerns in a desert environment.
Securing a shelter close to a water source can be your
best means of surviving in such a harsh environment.

The surface of the desert can be painfully hot. Sitting
about 15 inches (40 cm) above it can make a big
difference. Likewise, burrowing or trenching about the
same distance below the surface can be equally cooling.
Shading the trench further cools your immediate
environment.

Suppose you've decided to take a shortcut in your car
through the desert. Highway signs warn you that there are
no services whatsoever for the next 83 miles (133 km).

You head out, confident that you are in a well-running vehicle and you're only about an hour and a half driving time away from services.

A half hour later you decide to investigate a ghost town shown on your road map. It's only 10 miles (16 km) down a side road.

All is well until suddenly a dense, sweet-smelly cloud of steam spews out from under the hood. You stop the car, and before you even undo the latch you know that you've sprung a major leak in a hose, or worse.

It's midday, 110°F (43°C) in the desert, and you are 4 miles (6.4 km) from a road that has no services for 30 miles (48 km). There are no trees, no rock outcroppings, nothing. The ghost town could provide shelter, but even if it's still standing, it's a good 6 miles (9.6 km) away. What to do?

You can remain in your vehicle, but it will quickly become an unbearable oven on wheels as the sun bakes its metal exterior. Using your survival sense, you decide to first drink some of the water you have with you, and you collect extra water for later.

The next thing you do is dig out a space under the car where you can wait out the hot sun of daylight. You make a wide trench perpendicular to the rear bumper (the front of the car doesn't offer as much clearance as the back) and slide under the car. Your ordeal is  long from over, but at least you have dealt with the critical conditions at the onset of your dilemma.

If you are in a situation without a vehicle but have a poncho or there is adequate brush around, you can create a shade shelter in the ground. Make a trench long and wide enough to recline. Along each long side of the trench make a raised support ridge using rocks, sand or long branches.

You want to build up the sides of the trench so you can put a shade layer across the trench. This layer can be a poncho, tarp, whatever may be available. It may just be a layer of leafed branches from nearby sagebrush. Ideally this should be dense enough to provide shade. If you have a second tarp, you can lay it over this shade layer, securing it in place. Your trench should at least make the heat bearable.

The need for warmth in the desert becomes evident at night. Be prepared by gathering whatever can be used for insulation and to build a fire. Be especially cautious of the creatures of the desert. They don't like the sun any more than you do, and your shelter may be very hospitable to several of them during the day and the cold nights as well. The plus side is that you might attract a lizard or snake— food sources.

Survival Tip: **Water Source**

Early-morning temperature increases may mean that dew forms on your tarp or equipment. You can wipe dew off a surface and ring out or suck out the moisture. It's a modest but potentially life-saving water source.

HOW TO BUILD

A key skill used in many shelter constructions is lashing—

using cordage or other materials to tie support poles together. Before you can start lashing, however, you have to have cordage and know how to use it.

Cordage

I carry several 50-foot-long (15-m) sections of cordage throughout my gear. Even my camera bag has a small ball of nylon parachute cord stuffed away for safe keeping. Natural cordage can be created from the fibrous roots and barks of many plants. Since prehistoric times, plant fibers (for example, hemp) and animal skins (leather thongs, sinew) have been used to secure framework to make weapons and attach skins together for clothing or shelters. Today, technology gives us fibers drawn from solutions in test tubes and enhanced natural fibers to create myriad forms of cordage.

In a survival situation, you may have to find or create fibers that can be connected to form small cords that can then be spun into longer sections to be used as rope or fishing line. Strips of cloth, boot laces and other materials also can be fashioned into suitable lengths of cordage.

Multiple-stranded rope can be a real lifesaver. In terms of salvaged pieces of rope found on a beach, for example, even a couple of feet of 1-inch-diameter (2.5-cm) sisal rope can be unwoven into smaller bundles of fibers, rewoven or connected with knots and used for fishing line, sewing material for shelter or clothing, or lashing and binding heavier loads.

The rope I carry with me is commonly called parachute cord. It's about ⅛ inch (3 mm) in diameter and is very strong. It's the perfect size for most field lashing needs and, when doubled or tripled, can sustain incredible weights. To keep it

handy, I wrap an extra amount around my backpack frame, make mini bundles to stash throughout my gear and have even braided it and used it for a makeshift strap on a shoulder bag.

Authentic parachute cord has an outer sheath covering several inner strands. These inner strands can be further separated to a single strand and used for fishing line or other small detail needs. Imitation "parachute" cord is merely a woven tube of fibers containing no inner core. Natural fibers can be found in a variety of plants common to forests and prairies. A widely-used source of fibers for rope and basket weaving is the root of the spruce tree. Native Americans gathered long sections of this root that grows right under the surface, formed them into a coil and used the hot coals of a fire to burn off the outer skin of the root. The exposed root was then used to tie together other tools and materials—or woven to form baskets, mats and other items.

A form of Chinese elm that grows wild in woodlots has a bark that easily peels in long strips and makes adequate binding cordage for modest load-bearing lashings. Some grasses are strong enough for their blades to be used for simple, temporary wraps, too.

Some cordage frays easily when cut. "Whipping" the end of a frayed rope is a technique used to keep the rope from unraveling more. It's also a good preventative treatment immediately upon cutting a new end to a rope.

Synthetic cordage can also become frayed when cut. If the cordage is composed of an inner and outer sleeve, each may unravel at different rates, causing all kinds of problems. To hold fast the end of a synthetic rope, melt the frayed end with a flame to burn off excess material, and then form the melted or softened material into a blunt or tapered end no larger than the diameter of the cordage.

Knots

Once you have a supply of cordage, the next step in survival skills development is knowing a few common knots that work in a variety of situations. Knots can be used to join two lengths of rope together or they can be used to secure one object to another. Here are the most common knots you may need and their typical applications:

Square/Reef: Basically a double-overhand knot, it is used to join two ropes of the same diameter together. The right end is crossed over the left end and then, as the left end, it is brought back over the right (right over left; left over right). Screw this one up and you've tied the "granny"—a completely worthless knot.

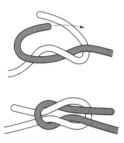

I use a square knot as the first knot in tying my bootlaces together. Once all the eyes or hooks are connected and the lace tightened, I tie a square knot to keep the lacing tight as I finish off tying the loops. This prevents snags from loosening the boot, even if the loop is pulled free. To undo the knot, pull on one end of the lace to straighten out the knot for easy untying.

Bowline: The rescuer's knot. This is used to form a non-slipping loop that can be placed around a victim's torso without slipping tighter. Used extensively to haul up victims. There are several variations on this knot, but this is the basic form.

Clove hitch: Used to attach a rope to a post or rail, particularly one with a smooth surface because the rope holds fast against itself. The clove hitch is often used at the start and finish of several types of lashing.

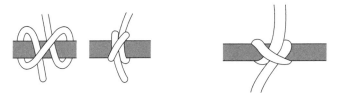

Figure 8: Looking just like its name, this knot (aabove) is used as a "stopper" knot to keep the end of a rope from slipping back through the knot or an eyelet. It can also be tied at the end of a frayed rope in lieu of whipping the end of that rope.

Sheet bend: This knot is used to join two ropes of different diameters together. It's handy if one rope isn't quite long enough.

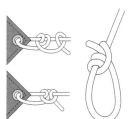

Tautline hitch: The tent-pitching knot (right), used as an adjustable knot to keep tension on tent lines as the hitch slides when tension is released, but holds when tension returns. This knot does not hold as well on some synthetic lines (two tautlines in succession can be used).

Timber hitch: Use this knot (right) as a starting knot for lashing. It can also can be used to tie a rope around a section of log for dragging (below).

Two half hitches: Another way to attach a rope to a post or pipe. This is basically a rope looped around a post with its end wrapped under in an overhand knot several times. Unfortunately, it's loose and not very secure.

Other knots may come in handy in particular situations. For instance, anglers know many knots used to join lines together or to attach lines to lures and hooks. Many knots used by mariners are variations on the basic forms. Those who haul gear for a living (truckers, for example) have special cinch knots to securely hold loads. It only takes practice to become proficient in basic knot tying—a good skill to have, even if you never need it in a survival situation.

Lashing

I once spent two weeks living in a camp where everything was lashed together: table frames, bench frames, lashed shelves that were then lashed to trees. If it involved more that two poles, it was lashed together. That was a Boy Scout camp and our lashing skills had been honed on a dozen overnights throughout the year. If you've never lashed a structure together before, you may be surprised at how secure and solid you can tie poles and logs together. Our troop once constructed a lean-to 8 feet (2.4 m) wide, 6 feet (1.8 m) tall and nearly 8 feet (2.4 m) deep using only 4-inch-diameter (10-cm) birch logs and baling twine. It stood for several months, with no further maintenance.

There are three main steps to securing a lashing:
1. Determine where the cross members will go, and secure the leading end of your lashing cordage to one pole using a timber hitch or clove hitch.
2. Make at least three primary wraps around the members depending on the type of lash or structure you are making.
3. Close off the lash by securing the end of the remaining rope in a clove hitch on the opposite member from the leading knot.

While there are perhaps a half-dozen different types of lashings, there are two that offer the basic holding power needed to make a secure frame: square lash and sheer lash.

Square lash: Everything from the smallest twig animal cage to a large, load-bearing bridge can be constructed using the same square lash. This is the most commonly used lash, where the poles are laid perpendicular to each other, and each is lashed to the other using three wraps around each pole in succession. Here are the steps to making an efficient square lash:

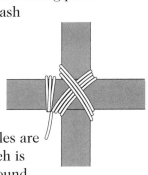

1. Secure one end of the lashing cord to a pole using a hitch knot.
2. Wrap the rope around each pole, in turn, at least three times.
3. Tighten the wraps around the poles by several wraps of the lashing between the poles, cinching those perpendicular wraps by pulling the cord as tight as possible on each wrap. Tie off the trailing end of the lashing cord using a clove hitch.
4. Use more square lashes to frame up the structure, each one will help the other lashings remain fast.

Sheer lash: This is the lashing used when the poles will be erected to form a Y, tripod or other angled frame. Here are the steps to tie this lashing:

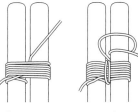

1. Lay the poles evenly side-by-side, right next to each other.
2. Begin the lashing using the timber hitch and complete at least three or four turns around both poles (sometimes you can wrap the poles too

tightly to allow them to open out, so be prepared to re-tie this a few times until you get the feel for it).

3. Once the poles are wrapped, make two or three tight wraps around the lashing between the poles—these wraps will be at right angles to the first wraps you did. Again, you are further tightening the lashing by doing this. Complete the lashing by securing the end of the rope in a clove hitch around one of the poles.

4. The two poles can now be spread apart and erected or otherwise used as an end support over a fire pit, as the ends of a stand-alone lean-to or for other needs.

Other lashings: A diagonal lash is basically the sheer lash, except that three poles are used. The middle pole is laid out on the ground in the opposite direction, its end overlapping the other two ends. When wrapped, all three ends are lashed together several inches in from the poles' ends. Each wrap between the logs is then wrapped and the rope end secured with a clove hitch.

This lashing is sometimes called the tripod lash because, once tied, the two outside poles are erected and swung outward while the center pole is swung out at right angles to the other two to form the third leg of the tripod. This frame can be the start of a tipi frame or, on a smaller scale with extended ends, be a three-point support for a washbasin.

There are also some running lashes, called cinch lashes among other names, that are a continuous lashing used to draw in the sides of a loose bundle or secure odd shapes and forms to a pack frame.

Practicing with twine on broomsticks or pruned branches is a great way to review knots and lashing at the same time. Knowing just the square lash can help you construct a fairly decent lean-to in an emergency situation.

ROOF OPTIONS

A shelter must have a roof of some sort. Natural shelters, such as caves, rock overhangs and even large, dense tree crowns can provide a primary roof. However, most frames will need to be covered with a waterproof/windproof material to make the shelter most effective.

The obvious choice for roof covering for a lean-to is a poncho, raincoat or tarp. Even parts of wreckage can be used to form key parts of a shelter. A door panel can be used against the windward side of a shelter or be the primary roof panel overhead. (Remember that leaning against cold metal conducts heat away from the body.) If wreckage or other materials are not available, natural materials must be found for roofing.

An initial layer of interlaced twigs makes a good foundation for a roof. This natural latticework can be leaned against a cross pole or tied or otherwise secured to it. The next layer of roofing can be more twigs with leaves, laid out side-by-side, row-by-row and overlapped as you would lay shingles on a roof. By starting at the bottom and working upward, you encourage rain to run down off the roof from one layer to the next.

Heaping leaves and forest floor litter on top of your lean-to builds up a thick insulating layer that also helps keep rain out of your structure. Finally, you might want to add more twigs and secure them so the wind doesn't start thinning out your roof.

Finally, stuffing grasses and other insulating materials into your shelter will provide additional warming opportunities for you. Remember to keep the shelter relatively small—but roomy enough to lie out in.

Chapter 5

Finding Water

Hiking along one of the trails that loops through the western end of Isle Royale National Park off the north shore of Lake Superior, four buddies and I met at an old copper mining site at a minor trail junction.

I had been rationing my own water supply during the hike as the temperatures in the interior of the island settled into the mid-80s (about 29°C). Sipping limited amounts of precious water, I made a point of leaving myself about ⅔ of a quart (0.6 l) for the 5-mile (8-km) trip two of us were making to our campsite near the park's Windigo Lodge headquarters.

One of the others had forgotten water and asked for a drink. Despite knowing there were no opportunities to refill our canteens between the mining site and the lodge, I reluctantly offered mine. I suggested that he only take a few mouthfuls and should use the group's water purifier to refill at a lake they would come to farther on. My request fell upon deaf, but thirst-quenched, ears. My canteen was returned with about ½ cup (118 ml) of water remaining!

I coveted those ounces of water for about 3 miles (5 km) before ripping the cap off that canteen and sucking it dry. Still about 2 miles (3 km) from any water source, my buddy (who had no water at all) and I developed a "cotton mouth" thirst and felt as if someone had loaded our packs with mine tailings while we had rested. We literally dragged our feet another mile (1.6 km) before we had to stop again.

I frantically looked through my pack for relief. After pulling nearly everything apart in my desperate search I found two oranges that had settled to the bottom of my pack. We nearly sucked the moisture out of the rinds! We returned to camp and consumed at least a quart (liter) of water each without stopping to gasp for air.

I committed at least four errors regarding any water "smarts" I thought I had:

1. I failed to ensure that each hiker carried plenty of drinking water.
2. I failed to carry enough water for myself.
3. Because of #2, I failed to consume adequate amounts while resting and instead foolishly "rationed" my water excessively.
4. I didn't even think of water until after I felt thirsty (a sign that I had already waited too long).

LOSING BODILY FLUIDS

Water is the essential liquid of life. It bathes our cells and is involved in myriad life-sustaining chemical reactions within the body, making up between 60 and 70 percent of the body's total weight.

One of the most common errors in proper water management of the human body is not consuming enough water soon enough. Often we wait to drink until we feel thirsty or until the color of our urine is somewhere between that of orange juice and iced tea! We might not even realize that the headache or slight disorientation we are experiencing is due to lack of water. When you realize how many ways the body spends or expels moisture, you become aware of the need to replenish that loss adequately and frequently. Here are some of the ways the body loses water:

➤ **Perspiration:** Losing water through perspiration is probably the most commonly recognized way the body relieves itself of water.

➤ **Respiration:** Simply breathing, the process of drawing in oxygen and other gaseous elements, warms that air and adds moisture to it. Upon expending that air, the body loses that moisture. In a survival situation, you can reduce that loss by talking only when necessary. Save your words and moisture, and breathe through your nose!

➤ **Digestion:** Less well-known is the use of water in processing the food we eat. Of the three main food groups (carbohydrates, fats and protein), proteins are the hardest to digest and therefore require the most water. A basic survival technique related to water consumption is to reduce the amount of food you eat if water is in limited supply. You can last a long time without filling your belly—but only several days if you let your body run dry.

➤ **Urination:** Urine and excrement are two other ways the body loses water. This, coupled with the need for water to digest food, is another reason eating should be done conservatively whenever water is limited.

➤ **Bleeding and vomiting:** Because of the high water

content of plasma, bleeding also draws water from the body. Vomiting poses another challenge in attempts to retain fluids.

Dehydration

Dehydration is the loss of water and vital blood salts and minerals (sodium, potassium). An inadequate amount of water in the body affects the kidneys, heart and brain. The most common causes of dehydration are excessive sweating/heat exhaustion, fever, vomiting and diarrhea.

Survival Tip: **Dehydration Symptoms**

Dehydration can be ascertained quickly by examining the color of the urine of the suspected victim (dark orange or extremely yellow).

Also, pinch the skin on the back of the person's hand. If that peak of pinched skin is not elastic and does not draw back to normal position quickly, there is high likelihood of dehydration.

There are three levels of dehydration, each with its own warning signs: mild, moderate and severe.

➤ Mild is when the body is dehydrated by about 3 to 5 percent of its total weight. Symptoms include thirst, dry lips and slightly dry mouth membranes.

➤ Moderate is when the body is dehydrated by about 6 to 9 percent of its total body weight. Symptoms include very dry mouth membranes, sunken eyes, skin does not bounce back when pinched and released. Some dizziness and lack of some motor coordination may be noticed.

➤ Severe is when the body is dehydrated by 10 percent or more of its total body weight. This includes all the signs of moderate dehydration, plus rapid and weak pulse

(100+ at rest), cold hands and feet, rapid breathing, confusion/ lethargy and blue lips.

Only mild and moderate can be treated in the field; severe dehydration requires hospitalization.

In its early stages, dehydration can be treated simply by giving the victim water. An oral rehydration solution (ORS) offers not only vital liquid, but also equally vital salts and minerals. These ORSs are commercially available and often used in the treatment of infants suffering from dehydration. ORS packets combine carbohydrate and electrolytes in powder form. Typically this includes dextrose, sodium citrate, potassium chloride, sodium chloride and possibly an artificial sweetener and/or a flavoring.

Survival Tip: **Drink Water**

Do not give a dehydration victim a "sports drink"—those touted as containing needed electrolytes and minerals. Such drinks can cause more vomiting and diarrhea problems, and their salts and minerals can actually limit water absorption in the intestines. Regular water is always a safe choice. Drink plenty, drink often!

Other remedies for curbing dehydration are soups, fruit juices, vegetables, herbal teas and flavored water.

COLLECTING WATER

It should be obvious that a primary preparation for any outdoor activity, whether it's an afternoon excursion or weekend trek, is to bring plenty of water—or be assured of a safe, reliable source along the way or at your destination. You should bring 1 gallon (3.8 l) per person, per day. And that's a conservative, bare minimum.

Because we usually need water before symptoms appear and because our body loses water as a natural, daily process regardless of any activity (called insensible perspiration), we always need to replenish water stores in our body. Where can you collect water outdoors?

The obvious places are the natural bodies we find in most environments: flowing in rivers and streams, collecting or percolating in lakes and other natural basins, or hidden within the flora and fauna around us. Some of this water is handily 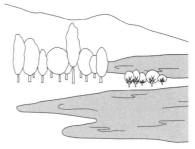 available while other sources have to be collected, excavated, physically extracted or otherwise freed from their captive states.

When first conducting the inventory as part of the survival thought process, think of all the things you can use to collect, direct or even use to dig for water. While a broken bucket can't hold water, it sure can be used to direct water flow from a tent fly into a basin or container. The hard side of a commercial plastic pail can be used to dig for water in a variety of probable locations.

Open Water

An important consideration when retrieving open water (rivers, lakes, ponds, etc.) is the danger of toxins and bad organisms too small to see—cholera and other bacteria and viruses, tiny worms and flukes and the ubiquitous outdoor bad guy, Giardia lamblia (beaver fever).

Even the purest sources of water—the swift-moving, rippling melt-off from a fresh snowfall high in the mountains—can be contaminated. I once was about to dip a cup into some crystal-clear spring runoff from a small, thawing rivulet, when I happened to look upstream a few yards and noticed an odd-looking stick poking out of a domed batch of snow at the creek's edge. As I peered at it, the image became more distinct. The "stick" was the fore-leg of a winterkilled fawn that had fallen into the creek and was then buried by snowfall.

A misconception I've seen published tells water seekers to select the swift-moving flowage of a small, clear creek if you must chance drinking unpurified water. The idea makes sense until you realize that tiny organisms such as Giardia are more likely to be tumbling around in that agitated water than in the settled water in a stilled section, perhaps in a small eddy or protected rock area.

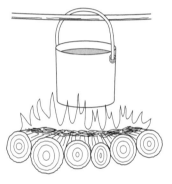

Better still is to treat all water from such bodies by boiling it first. All the toxins are killed at about 180°F (82°C), but since you can't determine that exact temperature without a thermometer, let it boil at 212°F (100°C) for at least 5 to 7 minutes, although continuing the boil for a full 10 minutes is added insurance. Once water is boiled (presuming it has already been filtered for larger impurities), you can enhance its flavor by rapidly stirring it or shaking it vigorously to reoxygenate it.

Survival Tip: **Keep Hydrated**

Should you drink potentially contaminated water if boiling is not possible? The main argument for this action is that many of the creatures that cause trouble take several weeks to incubate. Better to be hydrated during the survival ordeal (which lasts two to three days on average) and then deal with the consequences of infested water once you are safely home.

Other ways to purify water include using chemical puri-fiers such as several drops of liquid 2 percent tincture of iodine. Since some people have an allergic reaction to iodine, using chlorine tablets is an option that works. Commercial products have instructions for dosages, treatment qualities and time. Generally cloudier water and colder water take longer and require more purifier to be effective.

Filters can be made using sand, gravel, grass stems and so forth to get rid of some impurities, but these methods won't filter out the biological organisms. Some suggest using a purifier and boiling for safety.

Adding a piece of charcoal to the water improves the flavor by drawing some of those nasty tastes into the charcoal. Remove the charcoal, of course. Vitamin C added to treated water is said to remove all the disagreeable tastes. A small pinch of salt helps give flat water a more perky taste, too.

Rainwater

By far the easiest and one of the purest sources of water is from rain. Collecting basins sitting in the open or placed strategically at the bottom of a tarp or fly are fast, easy and effective methods of having a good water supply. Any surface that will cast off rain can be adjusted to direct runoff into creases or channels that will direct water into an awaiting container.

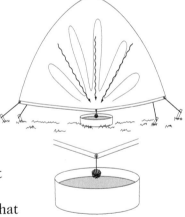

A boxlike framework of wood can be lined with a water-proof cloth and used as a makeshift collection basin.

Dew

Early in the morning as the sun warms the air, moisture is

transferred from the air to nearby colder surfaces. That water forms as small droplets we all know as dew. The surface can be a broadleaf plant or even the metal hood of an auto or aluminum section of an airplane.

The trick to collecting dew is to wipe those surfaces with a clean cloth or even a clump of grass. Once the material is saturated with moisture, it can be wrung out into a container or directly into your mouth. Make sure the cloth, grass and container are clean. I once collected a full cup (250 ml) of water from a 6- by 8-foot (1.8- by 2.4-m) patch of field grass in less than three minutes using the "wipe the dew" method.

This retrieval method can be applied to any surface upon which dew forms. If possible, make sure a surface is clean if you anticipate collecting water in this manner.

Plant Moisture

Most plants have water in some retrievable form. Plants such as those in the cactus family have a high concentration of water in the body of the plant. They can be chewed to release the water (do not eat the pulp; spit it out once all the water is drawn out of it) or squeezed to get the liquid out. Some plants will ooze water if they are cut, such as some vines, bamboo and a few others that seep out water over several hours.

Another method of pulling water from plants is to let nature run its course and collect the water given off by plants through evaporation. Have you ever noticed how a clear trash bag full of lawn clippings or leaves starts to form condensation on the inside of the bag? You can duplicate that effect with a live bush or section of leafed branches.

Ideally, you'd use a clear plastic bag and completely enclose the branches or small bush in the plastic. Fill the bag with air, tie it off around the branch or base of the shrub and arrange the bag so there is one low corner if hanging from a tree, or one corner farther downhill if on the ground. This is where the water will collect. You can retrieve the water periodically. If you happen to have several bags handy you can collect from several sources at the same time.

Like plants that are considered edible, those that are a good source of water should be researched and identified in the field before they need to be called upon in an emergency. Each region of the country offers different plants, and the seasons will affect which plants can be used when. Learn these things before you need to use them.

Solar Still
The idea behind the solar still is that moisture from materials such as leaves, grasses, seaweed or even clothes soaked in seawater will evaporate and condense onto a surface. If this surface sheds water into a container, you can retrieve this water in a survival situation.

➤ The key to making a still is to have a large sheet of plastic, preferably clear or at least translucent. It can be milk colored or slightly tinted but not black. This sheet is spread out beyond the edges of a crater dug into the soil or sand. The crater should be at least 3 to 4 feet (0.9 to 1.2 m) wide and about 2 feet (60 cm) deep. It is lined with moisture-bearing materials, laid out around the sides of the crater.

➤ In the bottom of
the crater, a
collecting
container is
placed as close to
the center of the
crater as possible.
Often the end of a
drinking tube is secured to
the bottom of the container. The
tube is then lined up the side of the crater wall and
extended beyond the edge of the crater.

➤ The plastic sheet is draped over this crater and spread
flat, just tight enough to remove all wrinkles and
creases. The plastic is weighted down along the edge of
the crater but is loose enough to allow the plastic to sag
in the middle. A small rock is placed on the plastic,
centered directly over the container at the base of the
crater. This causes the plastic sheet over the hole to
form a cone-shaped depression over the crater. The still
is now ready for action.

➤ The sun warms the chamber within the crater and the
heat and moisture are contained under the plastic
canopy. The air outside the plastic is cooler, so moisture
evaporating from the wet material condenses on the
underside of the plastic cover. Since the cover is slanted
(the weight of the rock on top forms a cone-shaped
depression in the plastic), this condensation runs down
the underside of the cover until it reaches the bottom of
the cone.

➤ Gravity overtakes the surface tension of the drop and it
falls into the cup. Once the cup has an adequate volume
of water, the tube is used to suck up the water, either
for immediate use or for transfer to a storage container.

Some survival instructors believe the solar still is a waste of time and energy, since it can be a long, slow process.

Ice and Snow
Opinions vary regarding the consumption of ice and snow and their conversion to drinking water.

➤ First, is the amount of energy expended worth the water volume gained? If you use body heat to melt that snow, what's the tradeoff in the time it takes to melt the snow, the amount of moisture you convert and the energy expended to get it?

➤ Second, snow doesn't contain the needed minerals and salts, so, over time, you are depriving your body of those requirements. However, ice and snowmelt water is better than no water at all.

Still, these seem obvious choices in the winter. In colder climates it will be the only form of water for several months, except vapor escaping when you breathe and talk. Lake and river ice is naturally fresh water as opposed to potentially salty sea ice. Sea ice that is gray or otherwise off-color and unclear contains too much salt to be consumed. Ice that appears crystal clear with a bluish cast is usually salt free.

Unfortunately, eating snow or sucking on ice, especially in a survival situation, can reduce your body's core temperature at a faster and more serious rate than it's going to satisfy hydration needs. Also, since this water can be contaminated with organisms that are not killed off by the freezing temperatures, it should be treated before it is consumed. Melting ice and snow in a pot by the fire is the most common means of turning the solid water into liquid. Ice will yield a higher ratio of water than will the same volume of snow.

Once the first clumps of snow are melted into water, subsequent clumps dropped into that warm water will melt very quickly. If no pot is available, putting snow or ice into a waterproof container and adding a large hot rock will usually produce water quickly.

If you are dressed warmly and want to add to your water supply you can carry snow in a flexible container under your outer layers of clothing and allow your body heat to slowly melt the snow. Once that initial amount is melted, additional clumps of snow will melt quickly.

At Sea

It must be horribly frustrating to be stranded at sea, floating on trillions of gallons (liters) of water and not be able to drink a drop of it without getting sick and ultimately dying.

The most direct way of getting fresh water at sea is by collecting rainwater. An alternate method is to wipe up any condensation that forms on surfaces and then wring that water into a container or directly into your mouth.

All fish contain fresh water within their bodies, so catching fish and chewing the moisture from their flesh and body cavities is also a proven method. Fish often will actually jump into a boat, and many can be attracted at night by a light on the boat. Fashioning lures and line will be a key task in such a survival situation.

Beaches, Byways and Beyond

A trick to retrieving water in the wild is knowing where it might collect naturally, relying on the forces of gravity, the impermeability of layers that trap water and natural depressions where it tends to collect.

Saltwater beaches, for example, may have stored water just up from the high water mark on the beach. Digging a hole into the sand and allowing water to seep in can result in fresh water lying on top of saltier water below.

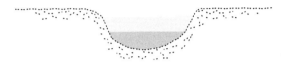

Groundwater can also be found in the bends of dried riverbeds and at the foot of some cliffs and rock outcroppings. Again, it's important to weigh the probability and amount of water collected against the hydration and energy expended to get the water.

Chapter 6

Searching for Food

My first experience with "survival eating" was during an outing with the Boy Scouts. Our troop decided to live off the land for one of our evening meals and the swamp adjacent to the BSA campground was to be our "supermarket." We decided that a batch of frog legs accompanied by arrow-wood or cattails would be our entrée of choice that night.

Our eagerness to attempt such a wild menu was helped by the fact that we only had to make one sample meal and—as every good Troop is always prepared—we had a bountiful supply of peanut butter and jelly to fall back on, just in case things didn't turn out as tasty as we all hoped.

One scout, Jack Jones, took the challenge to heart and returned with a bucketful of frogs collected in the upturned fold of his sweat shirt. We were (in hindsight, luckily) forced to eat the fresh killed frogs so as not to waste them—and found them to be quite delicious.

I learned two things that evening: 1) if you experiment with wild foods, you might be pleasantly surprised, and 2) if you ever get into a survival situation, make sure Jack is there, too.

There are so many unfortunate examples of survival cases in which victims endured for weeks without any food—or barely survived on insects and tree bark. Once the pangs of hunger and the psychological effects of not eating have been overcome (typically after 18-24 hours), the human machine can function adequately enough to sustain life for quite a long time. In an extended survival situation, those reserves, coupled with willpower, may be the keys to surviving.

In most survival situations, the reliance on food may be more psychologically beneficial than energy generating. However, knowing what's out there to eat and how to prepare it are skills worth developing.

It will be important as a leader in a survival situation to assure victims that the early pangs of hunger will subside and it will become easier to do without food. Meanwhile, keep searching and keep drinking water.

NUTRIENT NEEDS

The human body has several life-sustaining requirements: energy/fuel, resistance to infection, tissue repair, brain power/mental functions, comfort/well-being and the regulation of all body processes. To meet these requirements we need water, carbohydrates, protein, fat, vitamins and minerals.

Of those listed above, three are essential nutrients: carbohydrates, protein and fat. These provide us with fuel in the form of calories. Here are guidelines to the caloric needs of the human body, based on age, gender and activity level. These will vary with individual size and specific activity.

➤ 1,600 calories/day—older adults, sedentary females.

➤ 2,200 calories/day—children, teen girls, active women and sedentary men.

➤ 2,800 calories/day—teen boys, active men, very active women.

Carbohydrates
As a main source of energy, carbohydrates come in the form of either simple sugars (monosaccharides) or complex starches such as potatoes and breads. Starches must be converted to simple sugars, which, along with the existing simple sugars consumed, are carried to the liver, where they are converted into glycogen. Glycogen is digested by liver cells and passed on to other parts of the body.

Protein
Protein is essential for tissue growth, bodily repairs and the production of antibodies, hormones and enzymes. Humans get protein from meat, fish and dairy products as well as dried beans, nuts and eggs. The body requires a significant amount of water to digest all food, but especially protein.

Fat
Fat provides a concentrated source of energy—twice that of protein or carbohydrates. Dietary fat helps protect our organs. Saturated fats from meat and dairy products provide energy. Monounsaturated fats found in a variety of oils such as olive, peanut and canola help insulate us against the cold. Polyunsaturated fats help us absorb certain vitamins. These fats are found in corn, cottonseed, safflower and soy oils.

About 75 percent of fat's energy reserves are stored as triglycerides, representing about 10 to 30 percent body weight.

Vitamins and Minerals
Vitamins and minerals are termed micronutrients and are usually only required in trace amounts. In fact, too much

of certain vitamins can lead to vitamin poisoning. There are exceptions. An excess of vitamin C is simply discharged from the body.

Natural sources of vitamins are plentiful. Vitamin C is found in certain seaweeds, berries and greens. Young spruce and pine needles are said to contain more vitamin C than a standard orange—although they are not nearly as sweet and palatable!

Vitamin A is found in some seaweeds and berries. The B complex vitamins, as well as niacin, iron and calcium, are found in seaweed, crab meat, trout and fiddlehead ferns.

Survival Tip: **Rationing**

Although it is very tempting to nibble on energy bars and other emergency food in your survival kit, it's important to refrain from doing so. That food is for emergencies only!

However, it is prudent to periodically check your kit(s) to replace stale, dry and crumbly foodstuffs with fresher items.

PLANTS AS FOOD

The cardinal rule of natural food in a survival situation is: If you don't know what it is, don't eat it! That includes identifying it but not being sure if it's safe or hazardous. You must know what it is before you eat it. There are several ways to field test whether food is safe for human consumption. These take at least 24 hours to complete. The basic field tasting test involves sampling a very small portion of only one part of a plant at a time. Sometimes the raw roots of a plant are edible while the cooked leaves are poisonous—or vice versa!

After sampling a small amount, wait at least eight hours to determine any ill effects or ramifications from ingesting that amount. Then move on to another section of the plant and repeat the process. It's a slow way to go, but it can help you learn which plants you can rely on as a food source.

If you learn nothing more about edible plants—and animals—know this: Being edible does not mean that it tastes good. It may taste awful, repulsive and nearly impossible to swallow. However, there is a nutritional value, and it won't kill you or make you physically ill. Fortunately, some plants have very pleasant flavors and can be harvested to complement meals at home throughout the year.

Most plant identification manuals offer a section on the medical and food uses as part of each plant's overall description. Some of this information is based on historic and native cultural uses. Some are companion plants for commercial foods we eat every day, and some are unusual types that have a special tasty feature unlike all others. It is well worth the time of anyone who enjoys the outdoors to make an effort to learn some of these plants.

Another challenge in relying on plants as a food source is that they are, by nature, seasonal and regional. Many plants are only edible during certain seasons, perhaps offering their tender, green shoots only during very early spring. The rest of the year those same plant parts may be tough, rough and much less edible or completely inedible. Others that offer a root tuber are mature at the end of summer. Most berries aren't ripe until late July or August, and by September are spent or eaten. Knowing the seasonality of food plant sources is critical to survival.

Learn about plants in your area first, and then in the areas you will travel. When learning plants, don't just concentrate on the flowers in bloom—they appear only for a limited time. Learn leaf shapes, growth patterns, relative size of the plant and typical growing locations (low, wet; high, dry).

Most importantly, to truly verify a plant's identity, learn its Latin name. The same species of plant can have several common names in different parts of the country and sometimes even the same region. Also, different plants may share a common name in different regions.

Survival Tip: **Spices**

Many people carry spices and taste enhancers in their survival kits. Many Coast Guard air personnel in Alaska carry a small bottle of hot pepper sauce in their kits to make things a little more palatable.

On Land
Here is a brief list of some common edible plants:

> ➤ **Arrowhead:** This marsh-growing broadleaf plant has a leaf shaped just like an arrowhead at the end of a 2-foot to 3-foot (0.6-m to 0.9-m) stalk and grows at the edge of

swamps and marshy areas, making it relatively easy to harvest from the dry edges of the shoreline. It produces a narrow, white, starchy tuber at its base that can be boiled or roasted.

➤ **Berries:** Most red and blue berries are edible. Avoid white or cream-colored berries. Edible berries grow throughout most areas of North America. Some bush berries such as snowberries and elderberries are edible but can be way too tart.

➤ **Cactus:** I've only eaten the prickly pear cactus of the southwest United States and Mexico (called nopales; it's readily available in markets as a standard food item). The prickly pear has a wonderfully flavored fruiting body (the "pear") that is a good source of water, too. The flesh of this cactus, once dethorned, can be sliced into long, narrow strips and boiled or steamed and eaten just like a green bean.

➤ **Cattails:** What a multitalented plant: food source and insulation/tinder source. The young, white root tips taste a bit like potatoes and can be cooked the same way. The inner core of the base root has a spongy outer layer that must be peeled away. Collect them in early spring or late fall.

The new, green spikes at the top of the plant can be prepared like corn on the cob. Even the pollen can be shaken out of the flower spike and used as an additive for its nutritional value.

➤ **Dandelion:** This common and unwanted weed of suburban lawns is a delicious plant. Popeye would love it! It tastes just like spinach when cooked—or when its young leaves are mixed into a tossed salad. Like most greens, the leaves of the dandelion should be boiled for a few minutes, that water changed and the leaves boiled again. This gets rid of the bitter flavors. The tender new growth or those newer leaves near the center of larger plants are best.

Survival Tip: Milkweed Plant

Plants with milky sap should almost never be eaten. One of the very few exceptions is the milkweed plant.

➤ **Milkweed:** This is another versatile plant, offering food in the form of its immature seed pod, young shoots, leaves and flowers. These edible parts can be boiled for about 15 minutes, with several water changes along the way. Historical accounts cite that the flowering head of the milkweed was boiled, then covered in a batter and deep-fried to make a fritter. In addition to its food value, the mature feathery seeds also make good insulation.

➤ **Pine trees, inner bark:** The inner layer of bark on a variety of pine trees (birch, too) is edible in spring or can be dried and pounded into a flour additive.

➤ **Plums, other wild fruit:** I personally love the thick, pulpy juice of a wild plum. Likewise, but with much lower yields, the meat of the wild rose hip has a tart, apple taste (it is a cousin of the apple, after all). Rose hips can be steeped in boiling water for a refreshing, vitamin C–rich tea.

➤ **Wild asparagus:** This domesticated plant grows wild along country roads. Seeds deposited by birds roosting on a fence often sprout, planting small clumps of asparagus from one end of a county to the next. Keep an eye out for a clump in the fall and return the following spring to harvest the tender, young shoots.

From the Sea

A common saying throughout coastal communities is: "When the tide is out, the table is set!" Considering the mono/bivalves, crustaceans and other sea creatures that live in the fluctuating tidal zone, this area between land and open ocean is, indeed, a marketplace of great things to eat.

➤ **Snails:** These can be steamed and eaten by themselves or added to a sea chowder (toss in some seaweed, too).

➤ **Chinaman's hats/Limpets:** Conical monovalve tasting like clams—pry off a rock and add to boiling water.

➤ **Sea cucumbers:** Truly a gross-looking critter that is turned inside out and stripped of four longitudinal muscles that are then cooked and eaten.

➤ **Seaweeds:** While there are trace vitamins and minerals in all seaweed, it's not a major food item but can be used to enhance a chowder.

➤ **Sea urchins:** A delicacy in Japan, the roe of the sea urchin are a "scoop-'em-out-of-shell" treat.

➤ **Bivalves:** Caution! All saltwater bivalves (clams, oysters) have the potential for PSP—paralytic shellfish poisoning. If you eat PSP-infected shellfish, you'll die! During the Cold War, the CIA researched PSP as a replacement for the deadly cyanide tablets taken by U2 reconnaissance pilots because it was more effective and there is no antidote.

There is no reliable field test to know if PSP is present. Currently the test to determine PSP takes 24 hours. Some books suggest placing a small piece of suspect bivalve between your lip and lower teeth and waiting to see if you experience any numbing similar to that of Novocain. However, absence of a numbing sensation is no guarantee that PSP isn't present.

A last warning about PSP—animals at one end of the beach can register toxic in a lab test, while at the opposite end of the beach animals can be completely free of the poison. You cannot reduce or remove the toxin by cooking. It is best not to eat bivalves unless you know for a fact that the sand on the beach of their origin has been certified safe.

FISH

Freshwater and saltwater fish can be caught on hook and line tackle, entrapped mechanically, netted, speared and, in some cases, caught by hand.

A person handy with a knife can fashion lures and fish hooks from most anything made of metal or that can be shaped into a sharpened hook form. Lures should be shiny or otherwise mimic actual baits. Animal bones, especially those from birds, are well suited and sometimes nearly pre-formed as hooks. Simply sharpening a barbed end and attaching line to its shaft is all that is needed to catch a fish—using bait often helps but isn't always necessary. Lines can be made from clothing thread, thin plant roots or from strands of larger rope that is unwound and rewoven or braided into a serviceable line.

Knowing where to fish puts the odds in your favor. Consider the fish: It's looking for food, while hiding from being something else's meal. Deep pools, dark places beneath cut banks or submerged/overhanging branches and quiet spots in fast-moving streams are all likely places to seek out edible fish. In small streams, fish can be collected with nets or by using clothing or meshlike materials to form a sieve. Some streams can be worked so their flow is altered, diverting fish into traps made with rocks or sticks. Attracting fish at night with a light on a raft or boat is also common.

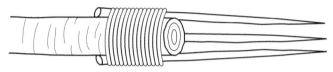

Fish can be "hunted" underwater in the ocean, as well as from shore in fresh lakes, with spears made from the long, straight shafts of soft-wooded trees such as willow. These are quite easy to make, especially with a good, sharp knife. The spear isn't used to necessarily kill the fish, but to impale it or hold it for capture and killing once it's retrieved from the end of the spear. Smaller versions of this type of spear can be used to capture amphibians and reptiles, too.

Even a good, old baseball-bat-size club can do a number on a fish rising to the surface or any kind of approachable food source.

Fish can also be filleted and hung out to dry—a form of jerky. Fish from salt water don't usually have parasites, so they can be eaten raw.

INSECTS

I've only eaten grasshoppers, and these were processed and canned in an excessive bath of cottonseed oil. I am convinced those captured and eaten raw or roasted couldn't taste any worse.

Insects are a great source of nutrition, although it may take quite a few to satisfy any hunger cravings.

Most insects are edible once the wings, spiny legs and antenna are removed. Insects that sting or are toxic are usually not edible. One of the more easily digestible ways to eat insects is to mash them up—or not—and add them to a stew or broth. Insects can also be roasted by gently stirring them in a pan mixed with small chunks of hot embers. Once cooked, the roasted insects can be picked out and eaten. It may help to cut off the head—not seeing a small, bug-eyed head staring back at you might make knowing that you're eating an insect less graphic.

Seeking out insects under rocks, in or under moist logs or even attracting them by a light at night are all common ways to harvest these mini morsels of survival food.
In the winter, check under logs and in the decayed centers of trees for insects in their larval stages.

GAME BIRDS
If you've ever hunted the spruce hens in northern Minnesota, you know how easy it can be to harvest some game birds.

Capturing birds by stretching a net across a flyway or chasing birds with sticks and rocks are both ways cited in some survival books for entrapping or harvesting birds.

One method that speaks to the bird's limited intelligence —at least as far as pheasants are concerned—involves a simple trap made from an old stove pipe or similarly sized hollow log.

The trick is to collect an appealing seed that will attract the bird. Scatter the seeds along the ground sparingly, leading up to and inside one end of the stovepipe or log. A small pile of seed can be waiting at the opposite end of the pipe or log. The bird will feed on the seeds and walk right into the trap. Since its feathers are all pointing backward from the head, the bird cannot back out of the trap.

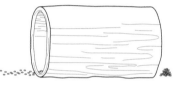

An alternate to this concept is to use a tube only very slightly larger than the bird's head. An enticement of seeds is again laid out in a line continuing into the small tube. Once the bird sticks its head in the tube it cannot remove it and cannot see anything approaching— including a resourceful survival victim.

MAMMALS

I find it very unlikely that a person is going to fabricate a bow and arrow and use it to shoot a deer, or construct a trap for small animals, without expending more energy than can be regained by eating the animal. That being said, you should try whatever works to get you through the experience. As long as you overcome the possible frustration of not shooting or catching a meal, the exercise can be mentally stimulating.

Most contraptions illustrated in survival books are worthy of the Rube Goldberg award for intricacy of design and function: "The animal runs through the loop, tripping the stick that releases the line that is held by another trigger stick that is likewise released when the weighted log falls, thereby pulling the snare tightly around the animal." At least it would be fun to build.

Seriously, there are dozens of such contraptions represented in manuals. Some are quite simple, others overly complex. There are many ways to entrap mammals, so perhaps it's best to work on those you can build with the least amount of exertion and those that will work for the type of animals in your area.

Many are ingenious, few probably work. I encourage you to practice these methods ahead of time—but be sure to check with local fish and game agencies as trapping may be restricted or illegal.

Chapter 7

Building a Fire

When I was a kid, one of the neatest things we did at the end of our Troop's primitive camping session was to enjoy a roaring campfire—out on the lake! No, not a campfire on shore that we enjoyed from the water. I am talking about a floating campfire that was a small roaring bonfire ablaze on a platform of grass floating on an aspen log raft. We'd tow the campfire raft out onto the lake, circle around in our canoes and toss a match to the pre-kindled fire. We may have even used a cup or two (0.25 to 0.5 l) of "boy scout juice" from our lanterns.

The point is, we were enjoying one of the most basic uses of fire—the pleasure of its company.

Who hasn't been drawn into "never never land" by the hypnotic hold of a blazing campfire—it seems to kindle a flame in our soul that has burned since humans lived in caves. Its use is one of the most significant events in our history. There is no question that fire is an important element of our existence and, when used properly, our survival.

Fire, as a tool, has many uses:

➤ It provides a steady supply of radiant heat for physical comfort.

➤ It provides mental comfort.

➤ It cooks our food, making most things easier to digest.

➤ It allows us to preserve food by smoking.

➤ It can be used to make tools by hardening woods and driving metals from ore-bearing rock.

➤ It can be a great signal for rescuers by the bright flame or bellowing dark smoke it exudes.

➤ It can protect a campsite from the creatures of the night.

WHEN TO BUILD A FIRE

There is no doubt fire is a vital survival tool, to be practiced and utilized. When to build a fire is open to discussion—particularly in a survival scenario.

The story in Chapter 4 about the group spending time trying to build a fire instead of a shelter exemplifies the issues regarding when to build a fire. Having a warming, drying fire is important, but if weather suddenly turns against you, it's better to have a warm, dry shelter than to be huddled in the rain, cold and shivering, hoping your meager fire won't go out.

If there are several members in your party, split the group and have the majority start building shelters—perhaps one at a time so if the weather does change, you all have the haven of one complete shelter instead of three half completed. Once shelters are underway, those building a fire can offer warmth to other workers. Also, once a fire is successfully burning, it is so very easy to use one fire to start others. Most of the time it just makes more sense to get a shelter first, or at least concurrent to attempts to build a fire.

However, this is one of those areas where common sense comes in. If it's already dark and you have no lights, a small fire may give you a better sense of the immediate environment so you can find the best place for those shelters. Also, if warmth is needed to treat hypothermia, one member may decide to start a fire while others work on a shelter and tend to the hypothermia victim.

Another situation where a fire right away may be appropriate is if you know rescue crews are on the way or that passing traffic will see your signal. Unless rescue teams were activated as a result of your incident (beacon signal or distress call before the incident) it may be several hours or days before rescue units even learn that you are missing.

Use your head, consider your options and start that fire accordingly.

WHERE TO BUILD A FIRE

Once the decision to build a fire is made, where to build it is an important consideration. Obviously you don't want to do what some have done: start a major conflagration that burns down a forest. Like any campfire site, you want to make sure the area is cleared of combustibles, that overhanging trees are at a safe distance and that winds won't blow hot embers onto nearby gear. On snow or wet ground, it is advisable to construct a platform of green wood on the ground upon which you build the actual campfire.

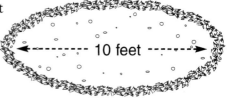

Since fires are highly visible, consider its location for those searching from the air or ground. You also want your fire to provide light and warmth to all members of your group. Prevailing winds may encourage you to build a fire on the downwind side of your tents.

HOW TO BUILD A FIRE

To understand fire, it's best to start with the three essential components needed to create and sustain a fire: fuel, heat and air (oxygen). Webster's dictionary defines the word fire as "the phenomenon of combustion manifested in light, flame and heat."

Fuel

Fuel is what supplies the fire with a combustible substance. Most often, this is wood, although any combustible solid can work (more on liquids and gas later). That fuel must be heated to give off a combustible gas that can be ignited and maintained until the fuel is consumed. To generate that gas, you must add heat to the fuel. That gas must then be mixed with air/oxygen so it can combust or ignite into flame and maintain that process throughout the expenditure of the fuel. Adding more fuel keeps the process going, assuming there aren't other factors that cancel out either the heat or the air from doing their parts.

Fuel can be classified into two groups: fuels used to start a fire (tinder, kindling) and fuel used to maintain the fire once started (larger kindling, logs, etc.).

Wood is probably the most commonly used fuel in the world. However, in many developing countries where the landscape has been chopped and picked clean of all wood for years, dried animal dung is a primary source of fuel for warming and cooking fires. Dried dung can be used as a source of tinder and kindling in a survival situation in many parts of the world.

Tinder

The smallest unit of fuel used in starting a fire is called tinder. It is the material that will receive the initial heat source and fuel the flame that generates the gases that ignite the kindling.

Tinder can be anything that will start to glow, as an ember, when a spark comes into contact with it. There are myriad natural tinders available in most survival situations. In the dead of winter, in a barren landscape, the lint compacted into the corners of pockets and within seams can be used as tinder.

The classic tinder is the papery bark of the birch tree. When crushed or cut into small strips, birch bark ignites almost instantly with a spark. Cattails, burdocks and other frizzy plant seeds work as well. Tinder can be larger sections of burnable bark, twigs and branches varying in diameter from a pencil to a broomstick. As the fire grows, so, too, does the size of the fuel you can add to it.

The most important characteristics of tinder are that it must be bone dry and have as many exposed surfaces as possible to be able to collect a spark immediately and then be coaxed into a small flame.

Your survival kit should contain at least one source of tinder. Scorched cotton (flannel works well) or cotton balls coated with petroleum jelly are two common tinders that can be carried in waterproof containers and used to start fires. Practicing with a variety of materials is the surest way to learn what works and how much effort is required to start a fire.

A handy way to become proficient at starting fires, particularly with starters other than matches, is to collect a variety of tinders and set small piles of each on a board or flat stone. Using your starter of choice, direct sparks to each type of tinder and see how long it takes to get a flame started. It's good practice for learning about tinder and developing your fire-starting skills.

Kindling

Kindling is the source of heat that transfers those meager sparks to larger flames and heat to start 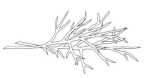 combustion of the larger fuels that will be used to sustain the fire. Try holding a lighted match to a wood board and see what happens. You might manage to create a soot smudge, right? Now, slice off a few long, thick slivers of that same board and try lighting them. These will ignite when held to a flame—this is kindling.

Like tinder, kindling is anything that will burn easily. It must be dry, and it should be collected in quantities large enough to not only construct a small fuel pile but also be in reserve so pieces of kindling can be added until the fire "catches" and is burning unaided. At that point, larger pieces of fuel can be added until the desired size and output of heat is reached.

Wood

Wood is the most common type of fuel for outdoor fires. Woods can be classified as hard, medium or soft. Anyone who has worked with wood knows that oak is 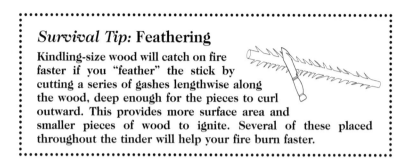 much harder than aspen, and that an ash tree is much harder than a silver maple. Pines are known as relatively soft woods, as are cottonwoods and willows.

Sometimes for a quick heat source, soft woods are preferred, especially those with a high percentage of pitch or sap. These types of wood tend to burn fast and furious, spewing sparks in mini-explosions when the sap boils and expands inside the wood. Softer woods, or woods with pitch, are good for a quick warm-you-up or to quickly boil water for other cooking needs. Their residual coals do not last very long.

On the other hand, harder woods are denser, so they burn hotter, slower and longer. They can create a good bed of coals for slower cooking, baking or lasting heat needs.

FIRE STARTERS

Mother Nature was the first fire starter, setting the savannah ablaze with a random, but well-placed lightning hit. It is likely that prehistoric humans counted on this natural act to produce fire long before they learned to create their own.

Fires can be started in several ways, most of which require a mechanical action where friction generates a spark or concentrated heat source that is then used to kindle a fire. That's essentially what a match does. Friction heats a solid chemical paste that ignites at a certain temperature generated by that friction and then kindles the medium to which it has been applied. That flame is then transferred to another kindling source for light or heat. Here are the most common fire-starting tools available and applicable in a survival situation:

Matches
As described above, the most common method of fire starting is to use matches. Of course, they have their limitations: unless waterproof, they won't light when wet; if they require a striker to ignite and none is available, they won't light; and they must be carried along to be available (obvious, but a factor compared to methods of improvisation in the outdoors).

Because most matches require a particular striking surface, it's wise to glue a section of striker strip to your matchbox—on the outside! A striker strip rubbing against match heads inside a container can literally burn a hole in your pocket, not to mention a king-size burn on your skin! The classic "farmer's match" used to be a "strike anywhere" match that was very handy. They are still available but some of them sold today require a striker, so don't assume that just because it's that big, familiar wooden stick match that it's the "strike anywhere" variety.

I remember a riddle that made the rounds at camp every summer: Imagine you are lost in the woods in the winter and you come upon a cabin. You go inside and find one match in a box on the shelf. You look around and see a candle, a lantern and a small wood stove with a small pile of tinder and kindling already prepared inside. Question: What do you light first? The answer is, of course, the match!

Having only one match, wooden or paper, would certainly generate heightened anxiety in most of us, especially in a survival situation. What if you have only one chance to light, and keep lit, one match long enough to pass that flame onto another media (tinder pile, candle, lantern wick)?

Remedy? Simply split that match in half lengthwise and double your opportunities immediately! You can usually use your fingernail on a paper match-sticks because the "stick" is made up of layers of paper that can be split lengthwise. Start at the end of the match and split the shaft. Peel 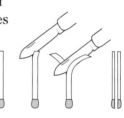 the halves apart slowly, working toward the match head. Then carefully peel apart at the head, creating two match heads where there was one. This is a very delicate match that burns quickly, but it does double your opportunities and makes for an easy way to ration a book of matches. While this trick works when forced down to the last paper match, paper matches are not really recommended for field use because they just don't hold up to moisture.

Wooden matches can be split using a thin, sharp knife blade or piece of metal. Again, care should be taken to cleave the match evenly, being very careful at the head of the match. On any match, but particularly those split as described, it helps to use a finger behind the match head when stroking it along the striker surface. This gives support to the back of the match and helps provide even pressure to the match head. It only takes one burnt fingertip to learn when to pull your finger away once the head is lit.

There are several wooden matches on the market that are combination wind/weather/waterproof. Some brands will even light in a hurricane! These "storm matches" can last about 10 to 12 seconds and burn very intensely, making them handy in severe weather conditions. One drawback they share with other matches is that they need a striking strip in order to light.

Watertight containers are also available. Matches can be waterproofed at home using paraffin wax to completely coat the match head and stick. Clear fingernail polish may also be used instead of wax.

There is one more tool that works well with matches: a commercial "fire stick." These are fibrous, square-sided sticks about 6 inches (15 cm) long that can be used either like a candle (using its prolonged flame to start kindling) or as a piece of readily com- bustible kindling to help spread combustion throughout other kindling.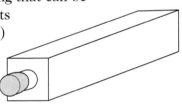

An old outdoor trick is to drill a small hole into the end of a fire stick and insert the head of a "strike-anywhere" wooden match (or any match as long as you remember to include the striker strip). The "fire-stick match" can then be coated in paraffin and used to start fires. You can economize and cut the fire sticks in half, and even add a match to each end, multiplying your options many times. One advantage of this "fire-stick match" is that even with the limited dexterity of cold, numb fingers or wearing mittens you can still grab the match stick and strike it to generate a flame.

Flint and Steel
Thousands of years before an English apothecary named John Walker devised the first friction match in 1827, humans started fires using one stone (and later steel) against a piece of flint to generate and throw a spark onto an ignitable surface.

A packet of flint stone and a steel striker was the pocket lighter of the day for many centuries. Even today, some survival instructors encourage their students to carry such a kit with them. The steel can rust but both are impervious to the elements, making them mainstays in the survivor's tool kit.

Magnesium Starter Kits
An alternative to flint and steel is the magnesium block, from which shavings of this combustible metal are piled onto tinder. A thrown spark hitting the magnesium bursts it into a brilliant, 5,000°F (2,760°C) instant fire! Magnesium kits usually combine both the metal and the spark striker on the same unit. They are small enough to carry around your neck or easily include in a survival kit.

Artificial Flints and Other Strikers
There are also fire-starter kits that use an artificial flint block or rod and a steel striker to generate a spark or a profusion of sparks.

Most of these units are considered a bit hefty for use in a compact survival kit, but carrying one or more with you will offer a big fire-starting advantage.

They can be attached to a lanyard and worn around the neck or placed strategically in pockets of clothing. One such unit, the StrikeForce, by Survival, Inc., produces a shower of brilliant, hot sparks that has worked on many different types of tinder every time I've used it. I especially like this particular fire starter because it doubles as a powerful nighttime signaling device. The spray of sparks created by the striker on the artificial flint is as brilliant to the eye as the flash of a camera! One quick stroke (doable even when wearing mittens) casts a signal that lights up the entire campsite for an instant.

These units are often offered with a synthetic fuel, a polymer plastic fuel tablet. This tablet is waterproof and can be trimmed into shavings that ignite instantly when hit with a spark from these or other units. This plastic fuel floats. In fact, you can actually light it as it floats on water.

Survival Tip: **Stones**

Instead of using a lot of tinder, build your fire in the usual manner but make a small cavity in the side of the tinder at the base. Build up your tinder and kindling as you would a regular fire. Now find a flat stone, about ½ inch (12 mm) in thickness and about 3 inches (7.6 cm) in diameter. Place the tinder shavings from a plastic fuel tablet on a pile in the center of the stone. Use whatever spark-generating kit you prefer and throw a spark to the pile of plastic tinder. Once lit, quickly insert the burning tinder into the cavity in the dry tinder under the fire form. This will burn long enough to ignite the tinder, and the fire is started.

Lighters

In my circle of outdoor enthusiasts, the cheap butane lighters sold at the front counters of discount stores and quick marts have all but completely replaced matches as a source of fire starting.

While they have their limitations in cold weather and when they run out of fuel, they are still very handy to have in the field. Their adjustable flame is convenient, and their ease of operation makes lighting a fire a done deal almost as fast as you can think it.

The lighters are all the same size, very convenient for buying by the case and stashing everywhere. There is even a mini-unit on the market that is about half the size of the regular lighters.

Of course, there are storm lighters that can cost well over $100 (U.S.)—not a price tag that encourages multiple buys. Obviously these are sturdier and work in much harsher conditions. Use them together with the matches and lighters already cited for a variety of backup options.

> ### *Survival Tip:* Butane Lighter
> Don't disregard that spent butane lighter just because it ran out of fuel. You can use the flint wheel on top as a spark generator. If you can break open the base you can cram tinder into it.

Friction Method
A more resourceful means of starting a fire when you don't have flint and steel, you are out of matches and you can't "flick your Bic" is a method even older than flint and steel. The friction method is the principle behind the fire bow and fire plow methods of fire starting.

These methods require the use of a mechanism to create friction between two pieces of wood, which generates hot particles of wood, creating a glowing ember that is then blown into a flame.

Most survival books show a person on one knee using a bow to turn a vertical stick so its end will be hot enough to create an ember. It is imperative to practice this technique to become proficient in starting a fire this way.

An alternate friction method involves rubbing a stick

along a slanted groove, pressing harder and faster until ample friction heat is generated to ignite an ember and light the tinder at the base of the groove.

Both methods take a lot of practice and work to be successful. The components are all natural and can be fashioned with a sharp knife.

Lenses and Magnifying Glasses
I learned at an early age how to start a fire using a magnifying glass and combustible material. It works in survival situations, too. But you don't typically carry around a magnifying lens—or do you?

If you have a camera, a pair of binoculars or even eye-glasses, you probably have the means of creating a focal point of sunlight on an object and heating it to where it combusts. In some cases it may mean permanently dismantling your equipment, but we're talking emergency actions here!

Interior lenses in a telephoto lens, for example, make excellent magnifying lenses for this purpose. Binoculars work as well. Glasses may be a bit trickier when it comes to producing a clean, tight focal point of light small enough to get hot.

A newer approach to the magnifying lens concept is the use of a Fresnel lens. These are the clear plastic sheets that are engraved with minute grooves that act as a flat, square magnifier. When used properly, the Fresnel lens will enable you to create a hot pinpoint of sunlight on tinder. The main advantages of this lens are that it's light, compact (lies flat) and won't break if dropped.

Other Mechanical Means
If a vehicle (car, plane) is involved in your survival

situation, you can often recover a battery and generate a spark using its terminals and wire leads. Wire ends can be touched together to create a spark or connected to over-heat the wire to the point it can start a fire. You might be able to rely on gasoline or other fuel to help with a fire, but always make sure you are well away from any fuel storage or leak from the vehicle when you attempt this. A strand of steel wool connected to the terminals of regular "C" batteries aligned in a series can be used to start a fire, too. It's the same principle of too much current flowing through wire that's too thin, thus generating heat.

TYPES OF FIRES
Here is a quick list of the various styles of fires you can construct.

Tipi Fire
As the name suggests, this is a fire where the kindling is stacked upright in the form of a tipi. It is one of the most basic patterns for constructing a fire. It's simple and allows free airflow from the tinder at the base up through the kindling sticks at top.

It's a great fire to direct intense heat upward, to a hanging pot, for example. It is also a good fire to build in smaller scale to start larger fires.

Pyramid/Crisscross Fire
This fire offers a substantial base with each ascending layer slightly smaller than the last until seven or eight layers of firewood are stacked in the form of a pyramid. If this fire is lit from the top, it burns down into itself for a lasting fire. Started from the bottom, this fire produces a good bed of coals for cooking.

Log Cabin Fire

This is a modified pyramid in that only the outer, supporting layers are built upon, the interior being filled with tinder and kindling to get it started. Scarcity of wood, or an excess of only larger, arm-size logs, might encourage you to build the log cabin fire.

Star Fire

This fire allows for low maintenance and long, slow burning or smoldering as only the ends of larger logs burn.

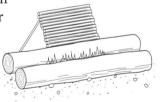

The ends of five or six logs are laid out so one end is at a focal point. Each log shares the focal point/hub and radiates out from it, like spokes on a wheel. A fire is started at the center or hub, and as the end of each log is consumed, it is pushed forward to maintain the flame. This fire is easy to maintain throughout the night.

Long Fire

Like the star fire, this fire can burn for hours with minimal concern or tending. Two large logs are laid side-by-side about 8 to 10 inches (20 to 25 cm) apart. A fire is built between the logs (several fires can be started along the log and burned at once). A third log can be placed lengthwise along the top of the two logs for added long-term fuel.

Hunter's Fire

I've used this fire for cooking for years. It's basically two larger logs parallel to each other with space in the middle to build and feed the fire. As coals develop and the outside

117

logs keep the fire contained, you can place pots on the logs above the fire for a handy cooking area.

Trench and Pit Fires
These are very hot fires that are either built in a trench (to protect against the wind) or use a trench to funnel air into the fire chamber from below. The fire is built in a basin with a trench dug out from the fire pit at right angles. Sometimes a separate chimney hole is dug so the fire is vented from a side chamber or shaft. A popular cooking, drying fire called the Dakota fire is a chambered pit, sometimes built with two venting shafts.

Reflector Fire
A way to direct warmth to a lean-to or other shelter is to build a reflector wall behind your fire. Typically a pyramid-type fire works best as it produces a wide area of heat that can be reflected back in the desired direction.

A slab of rock angled up facing a fire is a method of cooking fish filleted out on a rack or plank. The fish is laid against the rock, and reflected heat cooks the backside of the fish, while the direct heat cooks the front.

"Hobo" Fire
This is the name given to cooking fires fueled in a can or other similar container. Typically the fuel is pitch or sand, or cloth that is saturated in a burnable liquid fuel. The fire is made inside a large can that becomes the "stove" used for cooking.

Signal Fire
Although signals are covered in Chapter 8, fires can be used as a primary signaling device. An internationally recognized distress signal is three fires laid out in a triangle when viewed from the air.

Smoke is more visible by day than the flames of a fire, so billowing columns of smoke need to be produced when using fires during sunny, daylight hours. Fresh leaves and grasses, evergreen boughs, damp clothes and seaweed are among those materials that, when placed on an established fire, will produce smoke. You must judge the size of the fire and the amount of smoking material to use; otherwise, you'll smother the fire completely.

At night, the bright light of the fire is what will be seen. Crisp, dry material that burns brightly—dried evergreens, snap-dry branches and even flammable liquids work well.

If time and site allow, you can build three signal fires in a clearing, complete with tinder, kindling and wood already laid out and ready to be lit. Protect this pile from the elements until needed. It's important to be able to ignite the fires quickly in case of a sudden opportunity.

CARE OF FIRE

Fire, when used correctly and in a timely manner, can be a major survival tool. Fire building is an art form worth learning. Keep in mind the need to build a fire as opposed to creating a shelter, and weigh this, as you must constantly do in a survival situation, against alternative needs and opportunities.

Lastly, be careful with fire. Make sure your campfire area is cleared of burnable debris (including overhead), and don't venture off with a fire still smoldering. If you are moving to another location, consider a smudge pot to carry along a glowing ember. A piece of moss wrapped around an ember and then placed in a non-combustible container will work as storage for your "fire" while in transit. You can always add a bit of additional fuel to the container until you make camp again.

Chapter 8

Making Signals

A couple became stranded while camping in a very remote area of Alaska. They had no means of communicating their plight to the outside world and had told no one of their whereabouts. As vacationing visitors, they wouldn't even be missed for several weeks. After nearly a week in the coastal wilderness, the man decided to try his luck with a signaling mirror. He targeted the sky, the far shoreline and the mountains with flashes from his small, handheld device.

Overhead, on a flight from Tokyo to Seattle, a jetliner pilot spotted the flashes and determined that they were not random reflections of the sun off a boat windshield or even the water itself. He radioed coordinates to the tower and a rescue team was able to check out the flashes and find the stranded couple. Upon summarizing the incident, it was determined from flight records that the jetliner was at 30,000 feet (9,144 m) and nearly 100 miles (160 km) away at the time of the sighting.

Now this may be the kind of tall tale upon which urban legends are born, but rescue successes based on the use of a signal mirror are documented throughout search and rescue logbooks. It's just one type of emergency signal that can save your life.

By definition, a signal is something that conveys warning

or attracts attention. To be effective, a signal must stand out from its surroundings. It must be in contrast to those surroundings, as in the case of visual signals. And it must attract attention to be an effective audible signal.

There may be an occasion where a victim has little choice in the type of signal available. Conditions may prevail that prevent certain signals from being effective. Strong winds and storms generated by low-pressure zones may keep smoke low and in the trees. Flares may be too weak to soar high enough to clear a canyon's walls. Reliance on several signaling methods offers more chances that one or more will actually attract someone's attention.

An organized SAR unit is especially keen on looking for signals. They are trained to scan the countryside in minute detail and to look for signals that might typically be used in a particular region.

VISUAL SIGNALS
My first rule for selecting the type of gear I'll be carrying outdoors is that it's multipurposed. How many different uses can I get from one piece of equipment? There's an economy of weight to consider, but more importantly it helps me prioritize the "must-haves" from the rest of the

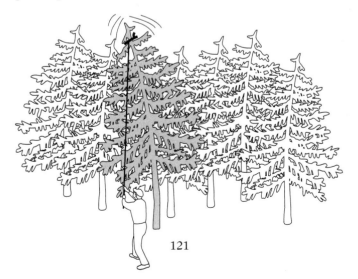

gear I've collected over the years. One of those key multiple functions is a piece of gear's adaptability as a signaling device.

Even a piece of rope can be an effective signaling tool. Imagine you are stuck in a stand of young to midmature evergreen trees, an entire forest of the same species and height. How can that sea of identical looking boughs attract attention? Get out your rope! If the treetops are within a rope-length toss from the ground, tie a foot-long (30-cm), broomstick-diameter section of tree branch to one end of a long section of rope. Throw the stick to the very top of a taller tree and try to snag the top with the stick. If trees are stout enough, you can climb all or part way up to secure the rope as close to the tops as possible. The idea is to use the rope to pull the treetop back and forth forcefully enough to make it sway. One tree amid hundreds swaying with little or no wind—or even against the wind—is going to draw the attention of a rescuer.

Bright Colors and Shiny Objects
These are highly visible and therefore make excellent emergency signaling flags. Fire-engine-red jackets then, right? Maybe not. Red is a warm color but one that doesn't stand out at great distances or when overcast. The highest visible color in daylight is blaze or international orange—also known as "hunter orange" in many parts of the United States. In the subdued light of haze, fog or the twilight hours, yellow usually stands out best. A Coast Guard buddy of mine said that one of the best colors to see from the air is robin's-egg blue.

Anything shiny can be used to reflect sunlight and be flashed as a signal—even a sheet of wet plastic. Bright rain pants or jackets can be hoisted up and waved at the top of a flagpole to attract attention.

Ground Signals

Some ground signals may be signs pointing toward the line of travel of a party that had to move from one site to another. Obvious signs are arrows drawn in the ground, sticks laid out to point the way and rocks aligned to form an arrow pointing a certain way. If you have a way to leave a message, it is very helpful to include the date and time of departure, too.

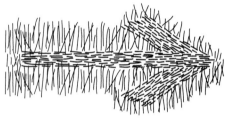

As part of a technique to both find your own way and to leave clues for rescuers, make signs along your route. This can be as simple as gathering upright shafts of grass and folding over the upper shafts in the direction of travel. Small pieces of cloth, a few strands of rope or even surveyor's tape (if you just happen to carry it with you) can be tied to branches along the course of your travel to both mark your way and to show rescuers in which direction you are heading.

Most ground signals need to be seen from the air as rescuers scan the landscape for signs of victims. This is why staying at your incident site is so important. It is much easier to spot a wrecked plane from the air (in most cases) than it is to see a small figure, even one waving his or her arms. The international signal for trouble is a big X stamped into the snow, laid out with branches and pine boughs or otherwise marked on the ground.

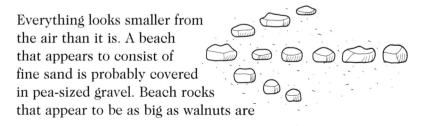

Everything looks smaller from the air than it is. A beach that appears to consist of fine sand is probably covered in pea-sized gravel. Beach rocks that appear to be as big as walnuts are probably the size of your fist. Cobbled beaches may have rocks the size of basketballs covering them. When making signs to be seen from the air, think big!

Markings should be wide enough and long enough to be recognized from high in the air, and at speeds approaching 100 miles (160 km) per hour. A general rule of thumb for ground signs is a ratio of 1:6. For every foot (30 cm) in width, the marking should be at least 6 feet (1.8 m) long. A recommended minimum width is 3 feet (1 m), therefore each mark should be at least 18 feet (6 m) in length.

In winter conditions where a solid, seamless snow mantle covers everything, you can create the illusion of large, contrasting signals by using piles of snow or other items to cast long shadows on the ground. It's critical that these signals be made perpendicular to the sun's path (aligning their longest axis north to south. Spruce boughs, cut and stuck upright in the snow, can be added to this method. Those dark-needled boughs work well when laid out on a snowy white background, too.

The most common and recognized ground-to-air signals convey specific messages based on simple, easy-to-make symbols. The universal "X" (unable to proceed), "I" (require doctor), "I I" (require medical supplies) and "LL" (all is well) are among a series of messages that can be conveyed this way.

Survival Tip: **Know Your Signals**

This is a story about the use of the wrong sign at the right time. It's a tragic tale of a survival situation that took the ultimate turn for the worse.

The setting is Alaska. This last frontier calls to a mixed breed of wanderers, adventurers and those who just want to get away from it all. Such was the desire of a lone camper who was dropped off by a chartered bush plane far up into the most remote reaches of Alaska's wilderness. The man desired to return to nature and live off the land for an extended period of time. Unfortunately, he made no arrangements whatsoever as to when, where and even if he was supposed to be picked up. Several months later, he realized his folly and decided to flag down a plane for recovery from his isolated camp.

Being so far north, he was off even regional flight patterns. It was several weeks before he was able to spot a plane and signal for help. So overjoyed at the prospect of being rescued, he made a fist and raised his right arm high overhead, waving or shaking it at the pilot who had swooped down to take a look. The pilot read the man's signal clearly and flew off.

While the man was exuberantly gesturing with joy that he would finally be rescued, his hand signal was the gesture specifically used in ground-to-air communication signals to mean: "I am OK." Several months later the man's campsite was found. The discoverers found a diary, which contained the entire episode with the plane. His despair at not being rescued caused him to take his own life a short while later.

Fire

Fire plays an important role in signaling. By day, the billowing smoke of three fires is a known emergency signal. By night, a brightly burning, fiery threesome works best.

Some books say that six fires are the international signal. You could compromise and make two sets of three.

Hand and Arm Signals

There is also a series of hand/arm signals that can be used from the ground to direct aircraft. Shown here are: "All is well" (top left); "Pick us up" (top right); "No" (middle); "Yes" (bottom). The messages are similar to the land markings and may also include other messages more specific to the conditions of the landing site and such.

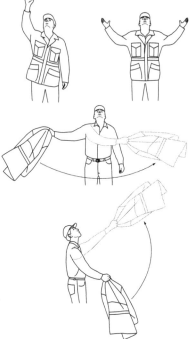

Mirror

Anything that can throw back the bright light of the sun can be used as a reflective signal mirror. Commercially these devices are made of either glass or of lighter, unbreakable Lexan (it also floats!). A pot lid, pane of glass or any shiny surface will work, but not as good as a signal mirror.

Survival Tip: **Mirror**

Signaling mirrors are relatively inexpensive, so each member of your group should have one. Some are no bigger than a playing card although the larger 3- by 5-inch (7.6- by 12-cm) mirrors are easier to handle. As a solo survival victim, having two mirrors available to you gives you an extra pair of eyes when conducting a personal injury survey. You might have a hard-to-see injury in the small of your back or the back of your head. Holding the mirror over the suspected injury and casting its reflected image to another mirror held in front of you will enable you to check out your backside.

The mirror works by reflecting a bright beam of sunlight off its front surface and toward a target—a rescue helicopter, for instance. To aid in focusing that beam of sunlight onto the target, a sighting window is located at the center of the rectangular mirror. The user holds the back of the mirror up to his or her eye and aims by looking through the hole in the center of the mirror. Once the mirror is aligned so the rays of the sun are reflecting off of its front, reflective surface, the user will see a circle of light. The user then moves the mirror to a position where that circle of light is on top of the target in the distance. When aimed properly, a person operating the target will see a brilliant sun flash from the mirror.

An alternate way to aim with a mirror is to use your non-mirror hand as an intermediate target. Here's how that works: Bring the signal mirror up to your aiming eye. Extend your other hand out to arm's length and make the "thumbs-up" gesture. Use your thumb to sight in the target (cover the target with your thumbnail or sit the target right on top of your thumb). Now take the mirror and rotate it until the bright window of light hits your extended thumb. Keeping your thumb on the target while the sunlight is reflecting off your thumb means that the signal is being flashed at that target.

Some signal mirrors have a second mirror on the backside with a red background. This is to be used at night with a flashlight to make red flashes visible over a long distance.

Two mirrors can be used to send a signal to a target also facing the sun (behind the signaler). This is achieved by using one mirror as before, but the target is another mirror held facing the sender and casting the flash of light behind the sender.

Flare

A common type of signal is the aerial flare. These offer a signal visible from varying distances in the air, notably to help a search party zero in on the signaler's location. Flares come in a variety of sizes and strengths, usually based on height capabilities and signal strength (intensity and length of effective burning time).

A variety of sizes of flares should be carried to cover a range of needs. A survival victim must decide which flare to fire first, and in what sequence based on flare time and distance from the rescuers.

➤ The brightest flares are the rocket parachute variety that can be seen for nearly 50 miles (80.5 km). These flares reach an altitude of 1,000 feet (305 m) and can last well over a minute. As they descend to earth, they are carried on air currents, so prudent rescuers will presume that victims are upwind (as most flares and smoke would indicate).

➤ The second largest flare is the meteor flare. The trail of this flare looks like a giant bottle rocket—a blazing ball of sparks and flame with a string of sparks or smoke behind it. These offer about half the effective range as the parachute flares and typically burn for less than 30 seconds.

➤ A popular flare kit used often by boat owners is the shotgun type of flare fired from a signaling pistol. These 12-gauge, shell-size flares offer about 75 percent of the effectiveness of the meteor flare both in distance and duration.

➤ The smallest flares are called pencil meteor flares and can vary in size from a ballpoint pen to a cigar-size, felt-tip marker. All are designed to be carried in a pocket or pouch. They are usually packaged in threes—and often, at least one of the three fails to ignite. Duds are more common in the cheaper and smaller flares.

The trick to the flare method of signaling is the timely firing of the various flares to draw the rescuer closer to you. Because of its height and distance capabilities, the parachute flare should be the first signal flare to use in most cases. (Obviously if the rescue helicopter is right overhead, don't fire off a massive rocket parachute flare.) The parachute flare attracts attention initially over a fairly broad area. It enables the rescuers to discern, for example, what group of islands you might be stranded on.

As rescuers approach that area, a second flare, perhaps a 25-mm meteor flare, would direct them to a particular island or bay. The third flare could be the 12-gauge flare to indicate on which side of the bay you are located. Finally, the smaller pencil flare could be used to almost pinpoint your location if they were flying right toward you.

It is most important to have a variety of flares and know their uses and limitations. It pays to learn how flares work and what they look like when fired. Contact your local Coast Guard unit (or police force if you are not near water) and ask about rescue flare demonstration opportunities in your area.

Smoke

Smoke is often listed as an effective signal, and having materials to create smoke quickly is an important component of rescue signaling using a fire. There are also commercial smoke signals on the market, used most often for maritime purposes.

Dense forest canopies or rock overhangs, low temperatures and erratic winds can all affect how well your signal is seen, so seek clearings for creating and sending signals. If you are using a fire to create smoke, be aware of the background scene from overhead or at an acute angle. Light backgrounds will require dark smoke (use gasoline, oil, rubber, tires, plastic or woods with high pitch content). Conversely, white smoke works best against the dark greens of forests, dark rock and so forth (use green foliage, moss, evergreen boughs, even wet cloth). Remember how natural Christmas trees burn so quickly and produce so much smoke? A small evergreen tree set ablaze in a clearing will create visually effective and stunning fire and smoke.

There are several smoke canister products on the market that produce a choice of smoke colors. The smaller versions, about the size of a large spool of thread or 35-mm film canister, don't last very long or produce a very high volume of smoke. Smoke canisters the size of a soup can last much longer and produce many times the volume of smoke. Be extremely careful when using smoke canisters because of the intense heat given off.

Lights

Other signal sources include regular flashlights, strobe lights and high-intensity lights specifically designed to flash or produce a far-reaching beam of light. Of course, these lights all depend upon batteries as a source of power.

AUDIBLE SIGNALS

An effective signal for ground-to-ground searches, and to simply know where everyone is in a group, is an audible signal. The whistle is the best-known type of audible signal—and is far more effective than yelling or banging on the side of a container (but that works, too!).

The only real requirement of a whistle is that it produces a loud, piercing sound with minimal effort. There are the classic referee or policeman's style (top), flat whistles (middle), spindle-shaped whistles (bottom), and a few space-age designs in between. The whistle's size and shape can be a deciding factor in choosing which model to buy. The smaller the whistle, the easier to carry and store in different parts of your gear. At least one whistle should be part of every piece of outer clothing you tend to wear.

The key to an effective survival whistle is simply whether or not it is a "pea-less" whistle. The classic referee whistle has a little ball, or pea, that rattles around inside the sound chamber and causes the whistle to make a twiddling sound, instead of a steady, piercing and often-harmonious dual pitch of a flat or pea-less whistle. The biggest problem with a whistle with a moving part (the pea) is that should the pea become stuck, the whistle is completely useless.

The sound created by a whistle carries for a long distance but can be hampered by the wind, other weather elements and by the natural acoustics of the area (thick brush dampens the sound, rock faces may cause an echo). Still, using a whistle will save your voice and lungs and generate a lot of noise with very little energy. Give each person in your party a whistle at the start of any outdoor adventure, especially children. Remind everyone that this is a signaling device and not a toy, and that three whistles in succession are recognized as a signal for help. Pay attention to where you clip your whistle so that it won't snag or get caught on something at a critical moment.

Survival Tip: Don't Wander

If you are sending any kind of signal, it's vital that you stay in the location from which you are transmitting. Wandering off after sending out blasts from your whistle for five minutes will only delay rescuers from finding you. Likewise, if you are on a roadway or trail and are sending a signal in hopes it will be heard by the victim, don't move for awhile, especially if you are in a car on a road. Honking your horn and then moving a quarter mile (0.4 km) and honking again is only going to confuse and disorient someone trying to follow that sound. Always use your head at both ends of the signaling situation.

PERSONAL LOCATOR BEACONS

Testing began in Alaska in 1994 on a device that is similar to the emergency locator devices on boats (EPIRBs) and those used in airplanes (ELTs). Called personal locator beacons (PLBs), the rescue devices were widely used throughout the world long before they were approved for use in the United States. Based on the positive results of that Alaskan testing, the FCC approved the use of these beacons effective July 1, 2003. Since then, search and rescue has become even more efficient and successful. Hundreds of rescued outdoor enthusiasts can thank a signal from a device barely larger than a television remote control for saving them.

These personal beacons link into the worldwide Search and Rescue Satellite-aided Tracking (SARSAT) system of satellites that orbit the earth and pick up special emergency signal frequencies. Here's a quick overview of how that system works.

In orbit around the earth is a system of satellites called COSPAS-SARSAT, a cooperative effort of the United States, Canada, Russia and France. These satellites receive signals from emergency transmitters on the

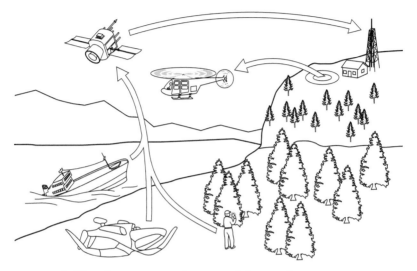

ground. The distress signal emitted from a beacon is detected by one of these satellites using the principles of a Doppler shift (the relationship of changing sound frequencies between observer and source when one or both are in motion) to locate the approximate position of the transmitted signal. This information is sent to a ground station called a Local User Terminal. From there it is sent to the Mission Control Center in Maryland, where it is relayed to a Rescue Coordination Center (in the United States, Langley Air Force Base in Virginia).

An attempt is made through Langley to contact the registered owner of the signaling device (each has its own specific signal frequency codes used to identify individual transmitting units) to verify that an emergency exists. Once it is determined that the signal is a legitimate emergency, the appropriate local SAR units are notified and deployed. Prior to 2003, an individual in the United

States had no such emergency signaling device legally available. PLBs are becoming standard gear for hunters, sea kayakers, backpackers—anyone who tends to venture off solo into remote environments.

One of the big differences between the existing emergency signaling units and these new PLBs is that those designed for boats and airplanes activate themselves, usually through the unit being inverted (a capsized boat) or by sudden and harsh impact (a crashed plane). The PLB units must be purposefully activated by hand. This places the responsibility for engaging the device squarely on the shoulders of the user. While accidental alarms are still more or less forgiven (although some want to charge for the services rendered during a call to the individual sending the false alarm), a deliberate false alarm can be punishable with fines of several thousand dollars.

One way SAR units can cull out accidental signals with the PLBs begins right when the unit is purchased by the individual. The unit is immediately registered, and each PLB has its own frequency code that identifies the owner of the unit. Specific information provided by that regis-tration is available to SAR personnel for follow-up contact. Part of the SAR process is to always check with relatives and associates once the identity of the unit is known, before activating a mission.

Depending on the type of PLB unit in use, rescue may be within a matter of minutes at best or a couple of hours at worst. The difference is in the makeup of a particular company's PLB product.

Each PLB emits on two frequencies: 406 MHz is used to attract the attention of the satellite and is capable of locating the devices within a couple of nautical miles. A second frequency at 121.5 MHz enables searchers to hone in on the target once on the ground. Some PLBs have either a Global Positioning System (GPS) program integral to the device or the capability to interface with a connecting GPS. (Be advised, not all GPS manufacturers make a unit that can be connected to a PLB). Using GPS technology as part of the PLB locating process, the units can draw rescuers to within 100 yards (90 m) or less—and at least four times faster than with just the PLB.

These units are small by necessity and style. Typically the units measure about 4 to 6 inches (10 to 15 cm) long, 3 to 4 inches (7.6 to 10 cm) wide and about 2 inches (5 cm) deep. Smaller units have been developed and are awaiting approval. These devices are enclosed in rugged cases that are at least water resistant, usually down to 3 feet (1 m) below the surface. All have an external antenna that either unfolds from being wrapped around the unit, extends from the interior or must be attached externally. Most weigh around a pound (0.5 km) and use a lithium battery capable of sustaining power for up to five years. They all work at temperatures to the –4°F (–20°C) range. Expect to pay $700 to $800 (U.S.) without GPS, about $200 (U.S.) more with it.

The PLB technology comes with a price tag beyond dollars. These units rely on the common sense of the user and the absolute need to activate based on an emergency situation in which life, limb, eyes or certain property are at grave risk. The use of a PLB should be a last-minute action after all other options have failed. Ideally, the PLB program will help validate real cases quickly and accurately so that many more lives will be saved. It must be noted, however, that as good as the PLBs are, like other electronic devices, they are worthless without batteries. Always carry spares, be prepared to deal with alternative signaling devices and always leave a detailed plan with someone in case of such emergencies.

Chapter 9

Developing Navigation Skills

Y ou know where and what the North Pole is. You know that the equator is an imaginary line of latitude, a base line around the middle of our globe. You also know that navigation means using tools and knowledge to plot and traverse a course, usually across unknown territory or through areas that require specific knowledge.

With this general premise of understanding, this chapter will add some fundamental and helpful bits of information that can be particularly useful in a survival situation.

MAPS AND CHARTS

Map reading is a skill that eludes some, fascinates others and can, at times, confuse many. When properly understood and utilized, maps can offer so much information that they are invaluable to the outdoors person. The key here is "understood and utilized." If you have a map but have no idea what your location is, that map may seem useless. If you don't know how to find your location on a map, it also becomes useless.

If you plan to spend some time in the woods, learn to read maps, particularly the topographic (topo) and relief maps used for plotting courses and seeking new hideaways. Even road maps and gazetteers offer so much more information than the basic highway maps of ten years ago.

➤ A topo map represents the features and elevations of the land. Those elevations are represented by contour lines drawn at different intervals and intermediate lines to show relative steepness of slopes, heights of mountains and other features.

Spend some time going over a topographic map of an area with which you are quite familiar. Local U.S. Geological Survey (USGS) offices and many outdoor

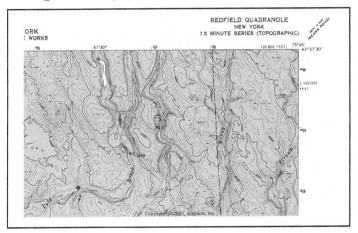

stores offer topo maps for sale. Go into the field and compare what's on the flat map with the corresponding land features. Each contour ring connects a series of dots that represent the elevation throughout the area. If you follow that line you could walk around the entire area at exactly the same level. Nearly every feature, structure and oddity of natural geology can be represented with a symbol on a topo map.

➤ A relief map does about the same thing only it actually shows the mountain peak, and valleys as images that appear almost three-dimensional.

➤ A chart is a map with some specific information associated with it. Nautical charts, for example, are maps of the coastline and ocean, offering geographical and geological information (rock reefs, ship wrecks, marker buoys and their corresponding signals). By the way, you'll never hear a real maritime veteran refer to a nautical chart as a map.

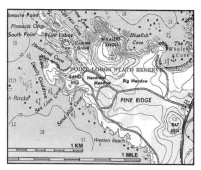

COMPASS

The compass has been a major navigational tool since it was first used on European ships in the twelfth century. It is basically a magnetized needle that, when allowed to swing freely, aligns itself with the magnetic field of our spinning planet. That is to say, it points north. Compasses come in all shapes and sizes, from the tiniest toy in a caramel corn box to elaborate base-mounted surveying tools. A prudent outdoors person carries at least one compass at all times. I have several stashed throughout my gear, many in the form of zipper pulls. I also carry a professional-grade compass for detailed orienteering.

The two main uses of a compass in a survival situation are to know where you are or where you are going so you don't get lost, or to plot a course if it becomes necessary to move from your survival location. In the case of being lost or temporarily disoriented, you can use the compass to cross reference distant landmarks to determine your location on your map. When traveling across unknown territory, the compass can be used to plot a course along a route. This method of taking bearings along the way, from one landmark to the next, helps keep you on course and enables others to follow your route more easily.

The use of landmarks is simple. Let's say you've decided

that you need to travel southeast until you intersect with a major state highway, at least 6 miles (10 km) away.

1. Turn the dial or compass face so your direction of travel is 135 degrees (SE or halfway between due east/90 degrees, and south/180 degrees).
2. Orient your compass so the needle points north.
3. The direction-of-travel arrow (also called the index line) should now be pointing to the 135-degree bearing.
4. Look for an object or landmark that is ahead of you a far distance and right on that index line projected outward from the compass.
5. Head for that landmark.
6. Once you reach that landmark, use the 135-degree bearing line again (after aligning the compass to north) and sight along the direction-of-travel line again to seek another landmark.
7. Repeat this bearing to keep you on course and lead you to your desired destination.

A basic course in orienteering will teach you how to deal with impassable areas on your line and other course alterations you may have to take.

If you don't have a compass you can determine a north-south line in the northern hemisphere using the sun and a watch. If your watch has a face with hands:

1. Lay the watch flat on the ground or other level surface with the watch face upward.
2. Take a small twig or matchstick and hold it upright along the outer edge of the watch face at the time of the hour hand of the watch (let's say it's 5 o'clock for this example).
3. Turn the watch face until the hour hand points directly at the sun. The stick should form a shadow that lies directly on top of the hour hand and passes through the

center of the watch face.

4. Find the center of the arc formed by the outside edge of the watch that lies between the 5 and 12 positions. That should be a point halfway between 2 and 3 on the dial itself.

5. Imagine a line running through the exact center of this watch, continuing through that halfway point on the watch's edge. That line points south. If you extend that line on through the center of the watch in the other direction, that is your north line.

But what if you only have a digital watch? No problem. If you know the time, you can scratch out an image of a watch face on the ground.

1. Draw a circle and draw the hands according to what time it is at that moment. It's best to wait until it's on the hour.

2. Place a stick upright on the outer edge of the circle you've drawn. That represents the current hour hand location on your "clock."

3. Extend that line across the circle to the other edge. You've just divided the circle in two.

4. Opposite 5 on the clock dial is 11. Mark it.

5. You can now either go along the circle and fill in all the time numbers or simply measure off equal distances or arcs of the circle and find the location for 12.

6. As in the previous explanation, you can find north by drawing a line that bisects the 5-12 arc at 2-3 and extend the line through the center of the watch. That line points north.

GLOBAL POSITIONING SYSTEM

What used to be the stuff sci-fi was made of is today's reality. We can now push a button on a unit no larger than a cigarette package and learn our location anywhere on the face of the earth! The Global Positioning System (GPS) relies upon a collection of satellites, 24 altogether, that can pick up a signal from a small device and, through triangulating that signal between two other satellites, pinpoint its origin on earth.

The user of this device can see exactly where he or she is located, right down to precise latitude/longitude coordinates. On some of the more advanced models, pushing another button will show you what routes to take to get back to a certain point or how to advance forward to yet another known point. These devices allow you to record and file favorite or significant ground locations by saving "waypoints" and allowing you to access them later. Your favorite fishing hole coordinates are a fingertip away with a good GPS unit.

In a survival situation, a GPS can help you find recognizable waypoints, or give you a big enough picture of your area to help you find your way back to safety and civilization. Remember, however, if you don't have a map, and cannot communicate to others where you are at, having latitude and longitude coordinates are virtually worthless unless you know your area very well.

As mentioned in Chapter 8 on signaling, some personal locator beacons (PLBs) are equipped with an internal GPS program that serves the primary purpose of registering those coordinates to bring the SAR teams right to you. Other PLB units have a way of attaching a GPS unit to them for the same efficiency and advantage. Check with your dealer because some PLB units and GPS units do not have the capacity to link with each other.

SEARCH AND RESCUE

The science and technology of search and rescue (SAR) have come a long way since monks and St. Bernard dogs rescued wayward travelers from the blinding, snowy, mountain passes high in the Swiss Alps.

Today search and rescue is a disciplined science with specific tasks and routines repeatedly used and improved upon in the field. The rescue techniques of modern mountain-climbing groups have been at the forefront of advances in SAR tactics.Years of experience with people of all ages in unimaginable situations have taught SAR groups valuable lessons in victim survival actions and reactions. Based on terrain, the age of the victim and other contributing factors, a good SAR group can, with high probability, narrow down areas of likely recovery for each mission. For example, on flat terrain, more than 70 percent of younger children are found within about a half-mile (0.8 km) of their last seen position.

The basic search and rescue mission has four distinct phases:

1. Locate the victim.
2. Reach the victim.
3. Stabilize the victim.
4. Evacuate the victim.

These are broad variables that change with every rescue effort. Sometimes the "locate" and "reach" events happen simultan-eously. At other times the location may take hours or days, while the "reach" through "evacuate" time is a matter of minutes.

A successful search and rescue mission is more likely in a case with savvy survivors. Knowing how and where SAR teams will conduct their search can help you decide where to go and what to do to make your recovery successful in the least amount of time and hardship.

Search and rescue groups typically set up one of several types of search protocols. Some are based upon statistically supported probability as to where a victim might be, based on those factors already mentioned: age, gender, terrain and abilities/condition of the victim. Others are more subjective and rely on intuition, local knowledge and perhaps a little faith.

One useful method, developed by Air Force Colonel Robert Mattson, is to accept input by everyone on the SAR team, regardless of rank or stature, and then compile probability areas based on the collective ranking of each contributing member. Those areas are prioritized and assignments made.

The actual on-ground/in-air search of an area is usually divided into segments. Typically, a hasty search is made to either find the person before the ground teams begin their orchestrated search or to canvass an area to rule it out, thereby enabling search coordinators to concentrate on the most probable areas first. A more thorough, but still general, search method involves quickly screening a broad area with dog teams, aerial support and others to determine clues or leads to further

143

narrow down or eliminate an area. These searches may include common encampment areas or general routes of "escape" usually taken by victims: ravines, valleys leading to civilization, streams, high and open knolls or countryside, the tops or edges of notable landmarks and such.

One of the best ways you can help, as that survival victim, is to stay put, get your signals ready and stay calm. If moving is imperative, be prepared to leave signs or a message behind before you vacate your last survival camp. When moving through the country, leave trail signs or "blazes" so someone trying to find your trail can do so.

Survival Tip: **Trail Marker**

Any brightly colored ribbon or material hanging along your route will be a conspicuous trail marker. Some survival instructors suggest carrying a roll of surveying tape in your survival kit. These rolls are bulky but show up at a distance. Other signs include rocks or twigs laid out in the form of an arrow or extension that clearly indicates which route was taken. Some soft, smooth-barked trees, such as willows and silver maples, provide an easy surface upon which to scratch out information: direction of travel, time/date left, and so forth.

Searchers are going to seek out common paths that they believe a victim might logically use when either wandering through an area or while attempting to "become found." Natural trails used by animals often lead to water and are often a path of minimal resistance. Be cautious of paths that seem worn by natural elements such as runoff or avalanche. As advised for desert trails, be careful in ravines that can flash flood at a moment's notice, even from strong rains many miles ahead.

Consider walking the tops of ridges rather than through the tangle of deadfall on the slopes. However, walking downhill along a stream that enters into a larger body of water is often a good choice as developments tend to spring up near such natural junctions. Along coastal areas, reaching a beach or bay is often a good choice, as is reaching the outermost point or knoll high above a beach. Any clearly noticeable location that would catch the eye of a rescuer is a logical place to be as a victim. The best location, in most instances, remains at the site of the incident.

Chapter 10

Field First Aid and Natural Remedies

It's a beautiful summer's day as you hike casually down a forested trail. There's a slight irritation on your heel from the new boots you are wearing, but the downhill jaunt is pretty easygoing. A few miles (km) farther and the irritation is worse, so you begin favoring that foot. As you traverse some loose rubble along the bank of a creek, you step awkwardly, trying to ease the weight on the sore heel, and twist your ankle on a small boulder that rolls out from under your step. You stumble forward losing your balance and smash your knee on a rock at water's edge.

As you try to right yourself and keep from falling into the creek, you snag your arm on a low-hanging branch that reels you around and trips you back—stepping across the shallow stream and into a thicket of raspberry vines that entangle your feet and send you crashing to the ground. Confused, bruised and scratched from scores of tiny thorns, you are reminded of your ankle by the throbbing pain in your boot. You look around for a handhold and realize you've landed in a patch of poison ivy. You quickly scramble to pull yourself up using the nearest sapling only to discover that hanging in its lower branches is a nest of paper wasps.

Short of burning yourself, you've managed to inflict most

of the types of injuries you'll encounter in the back-country. Aside from life-threatening incidents such as severe head wounds, near drowning and broken bones, most of the survival injuries you may have to deal with will be cuts, sprains and wounds as a result of carelessness and ignorance. Dealing with them, sometimes without proper medical gear or applications, will call upon your reserve of basic first aid skills and even more basic common sense.

Everyone who is active in the outdoors should learn basic first aid. At a minimum, learn the basic types of injuries, what can happen if not treated and what you can do to minimize the problem. How well you do your part will depend upon your skills, the gear you have and how you use it.

There are many good first aid books and manuals on the market and many more that are included in sophisticated first aid and medical kits. This chapter is not meant to be all inclusive of the information needed to be a well-prepared "first responder" and aid giver. It is intended to help you understand the magnitude of information for proper caregiving in a backcountry or wilderness setting. I cannot stress enough the importance of taking proper and professional courses in field first aid if you have any serious intention of participating in outdoor, backcountry activities. Your life and the lives of others may depend on what you learn beforehand as part of your responsibility to be prepared.

A prudent outdoors person is wise to take basic first aid and cardiopulmonary resuscitation (CPR) courses available through local Red Cross offices. More advanced courses such as training to be a certified Emergency Trauma Technician (ETT), are invaluable for those who might lead groups into the field or for those who want more in-depth first aid and medical knowledge and skills to be a responsible first responder. Much of this chapter follows the advice of Buck Tilton, director of the Wilderness Medicine Institute of the National Outdoor Leadership School, as presented in his book Backcountry First Aid and Extended Care. It is included as the official field reference in Atwater Carey medical kits. Mr. Tilton is a well respected and leading expert and author in this field.

ASSESSING INJURIES

One of the first steps in a survival situation after securing a location out of harm's way (you don't want to create more injuries) is to assess the injuries of everyone in the party—especially the leader and/or primary first aid provider (if one is not appointed, it will probably become apparent as someone with that training takes the lead). A first assessment may be whether the injured person can remain or must be evacuated. Even with that determination, evacuation may be out of the question, either because movement would create a worse condition or because of a location where evacuation will be too slow, too dangerous or too long to have a positive outcome.

Taking a first aid course will, if nothing else, help you learn to assess injuries and hopefully stabilize an injury until the victim can be treated by professional help. Learning the basic types of injuries and how each can be stabilized will help you perform those treatments during survival situations when you might not even have the proper field gear to apply and will have to improvise.

Airway Passages

A person can last only about three minutes without air. An injured victim must breathe, or any other attempts at reviving or stabilizing him or her are pointless. The victim must have a clear airway.

Basic CPR training teaches that you should check for foreign objects and then check whether the tongue is rolled or slipped to the back of the throat, blocking the airway. The basic head tilt or jaw thrust (for spinal injuries) taught in all CPR classes is a basic, essential procedure to clear the victim's airway.

Do you know how to perform the Heimlich maneuver? Do you know when to use it? Preparation is key. Take a course and practice before you are called upon to use any major first aid techniques.

Breathing

A cleared airway allows the victim to breathe, to introduce air into the lungs. Signs of breathing include air passing through the nostril and mouth, and the rising and falling of the chest. Chest signs may be very subtle. Remove or loosen any restrictive clothing around the torso so you can make this observation and, more importantly, for good hand contact should you need to begin CPR.

If the person is not breathing and you've cleared the airways and mouth, you must also check for circulation. The heart must be pumping for the breathing to be effective. An easy way to check for circulation is to take the pulse of the victim—feeling the pumping action of the heart at major arterial points that are close to the surface of the skin. A common pulse checkpoint is the carotid artery that runs lengthwise down the side of the neck, next to the windpipe, and is accessible for feeling the pulse right at the corner where the chin meets the throat.

***Survival Tip:* Bleeding**

A cut artery will push blood out in spurts with every heartbeat. Venous blood flows smoothly and rapidly. Apply direct pressure with a clean dressing. Raising the wound above the level of the heart aids in stopping or slowing the bleeding, too. Because of possible diseases, it's important to wear gloves while attending to a victim with open wounds or when in contact with any body fluids.

Consciousness

If the person is conscious and familiar to you, the care-giver, protocol can be quick and straightforward by simply telling your patient that you want to check him or her for injuries. If you are unknown to the person you are treating, it is psychologically quite important to introduce yourself as someone who's there to help and tell the person what you are doing and why you are examining him or her.

If you did not witness the injury-causing incident, or circumstances and surroundings suggest other injuries, you will need to find out from the victim where it hurts and other basic information. Depending upon the level of consciousness, the victim may have difficulty responding.

The four levels of consciousness are:

➤ **Alert:** The victim can answer questions, knows what

circumstances befell him or her, and knows where it hurts. There are degrees of consciousness within this level that can be determined by specific questions (e.g., the patient knows what happened, but doesn't know who he or she is).

➤ **Verbal:** The victim only responds to voice stimuli and may react by turning away or otherwise avoiding the aid giver.

➤ **Painful:** The victim only reacts to physical stimuli, the touching of sensitive areas or a pinch.

➤ **Unresponsive:** No reaction at all.

Survival Tip: **Assessment Notes**

Even without medical/first responder training, it will be very helpful, once the basic first aid is given, to note important physical signs such as color of skin (and any changes), heart and breathing rates (get a per-minute rate by counting the pulses or breaths for 15 seconds and multiplying by four). Do this twice to get a reliable average. Repeat as necessary and keep notes to aid professionals once contact is made.

If you did not witness the incident, one way to assess consciousness and learn more about the situation is to ask the victim how many members are in his or her party. A capsize incident that washes victims up on a beach may have left others in the water. An avalanche may have buried other victims unseen by those first to arrive. Simply asking "Are you OK?" may sound comforting but does little to assess the situation. In most cases of severe injury, shock may dull or nullify responses.

Shock
Shock can play a role in many field emergency situations, especially when there is a great loss of blood, but it should be anticipated with any significant injury.

Treatment for a conscious shock victim is:

➤ Lay the victim on his or her back on level ground.

➤ Raise the legs and feet 6 to 10 inches (15 to 25 cm).

➤ Remove any wet clothing.

➤ Protect the victim from the elements.

➤ Insulate the victim from the ground.

➤ Maintain body heat. Warm liquids can be given.

➤ Keep the victim rested for 24 hours.

Treatment for an unconscious shock victim is:

➤ Lay victim on his or her stomach or back with head to one side to prevent choking on blood, vomit or fluids. Do not give the unconscious victim anything to drink.

➤ Do not raise the legs/feet.

➤ Protect the victim from the weather.

➤ Insulate the victim from the ground and keep warm.

➤ Let the victim rest for 24 hours.

An additional concern about circulation, particularly bleeding, is the likelihood that the victim may be in, or quickly leading to, a state of shock.

Spinal Damage

Moving a victim, ever so slightly, can cause serious and permanent injury to the spinal column—especially if it is already injured from the incident. The movements of the victim must be kept to a minimum, particularly any twisting motions that might change the alignment of the spine, especially if it is already out of line, broken or otherwise compromised. Because the spinal cord runs the entire length of the spine, damage anywhere along it is a critical area of concern.

As a first responder, immobilize the neck and spine using a commercial cervical collar or makeshift one of available padding. Again, a good first aid course will teach basic techniques for stabilizing and treating spinal injuries. Being prepared and improvising as needed are the marks of a responsible and resourceful survivor!

BODY PARTS AT RISK

As a caregiver in the backcountry, you are going to offer help to victims that stops bleeding, allows for sufficient airflow, stabilizes known injuries and minimizes chances at aggravating injuries or creating new ones. Even if you've had no first aid training at all, common sense and an awareness of what needs to be done may save a life or make injuries less threatening and painful.

Abdomen

Blunt injury or penetrating wounds are common in the mid and lower torso. Sometimes the injury is not readily visible, so look for other signs such as blood in the feces, urine or vomit. Make sure the airway is cleared, repeatedly if necessary. Also, monitor the victim's vital signs as interior bleeding can quickly worsen the victim's condition.

Survival Tip: **Bandage**

The triangular bandage (or Boy Scout neckerchief doubling as a bandage) can be used to help secure large dressings, hold an injured limb in place, secure a sprained or strained ankle, or lash a makeshift traction splint. It can also be used as a sweatband or as ear or head covering for added warmth (stuff the bandana with insulating material for an emergency head warmer). If it is made of a bright color, it can also be used as a signaling flag.

In some cases, the intestines are forced outside the body cavity and exposed. Care must be taken to avoid or minimize infection. It is usually best to cover the intestines with a sterile material moistened with disinfected water. If, in an extreme case, it is necessary to stuff the intestines back into the abdominal cavity, do so with great care and then cover and treat the opening as you would a flesh wound.

Survival Tip: **Penetrating Wound**

If the object that caused a penetrating wound remains in the victim (a broken branch, a tool or knife), it is generally best not to remove the object. If it is too unwieldy, consider removing the bulk of the object without disturbing the penetrated portion. Unless the object is very loose, it is best to secure it in place and dress the wound and the object together. Removing the object can further aggravate the wound and cause it to bleed even more and/or cause other injuries. The decision to remove the object should be made very carefully. Get the victim to medical help quickly.

Chest

The chest area is usually injured by either being hit (impacted) or penetrated. In the first type, damage on the outside could mean more severe damage inside. A strong impact caused by a fall or something striking the chest may fracture a rib. If so, pieces of the rib could penetrate the heart, lungs or other nearby organs. Even if no internal organs are affected, internal bleeding can create the need for an emergency evacuation.

Some wounds require special attention, such as the "sucking chest wound" in which fluids build. Dressing should be applied so one venting corner is free. This specific treatment is covered in most medical/first aid instruction books.

Head

Injuries to the head can be as basic as a cut scalp or temporary unconsciousness due to a whack on the old noggin. As long as the skull is intact and the brain is not damaged, a wound to the head can usually be treated on the spot, perhaps with a few aspirins.

Serious head wounds require immediate attention. A skull fracture victim may suffer from an obvious depression in the skull, bruising around the eyes (markings reminiscent of a raccoon's face) or behind the victim's ears, torn scalp with visual skull fracturing or fluid/blood draining from the nose or ears.

Brain damage manifests itself with many signs, including deterioration in consciousness, slowing heart rate, unequal pupils, erratic and bounding respiratory rate, and headaches. In some head injuries, the airway can be compromised, so always keep an eye out for the victim's breathing efforts.

Neck
When assessing a neck injury, determining the cause of the injury and whether the neck could be broken is a crucial first step. Also, a neck injury that produces swelling can compromise the airway.

Rest of the Body
Injuries to the lower midsection and below are, in most cases, either broken bones or bleeding wounds that cut, rip, abrade or puncture (including all extremities). Surface bruises with no underlying organ or bone damage are minor by comparison and can be left to heal on their own.

TYPES OF MEDICAL EMERGENCIES
Most first aid and medical kits offer step-by-step information for treating injuries—either in illustrated booklet form or by easy-to-use information cards. In some injuries, common sense can prevail if no "official" treatment is known. Still, being prepared and anticipating certain types of injuries based upon the makeup of the party (for

example, curious kids and bee stings or older hikers and strains or sprains) can help you when you face an emergency.

Bites and Stings

Insect bites, though often painful, are rarely deadly. Diseases are transmitted by some insects even here in North America. (West Nile disease by mosquitoes and Lyme disease by ticks are two examples.) For the most part, insect bites are painful in the short term and a recurring nuisance at certain times of the year and in certain areas.

Using proper insect repellents such as those containing DEET, wearing dark clothing, closing off shirt sleeves and pants cuffs to prevent insects from getting under clothing and even resorting to wearing annoying mesh insect nets over the head are all common ways to fight an onslaught of pesky insects.

Survival Tip: **Bee Sting**

Apply mud to a sting. The cooling effect of mud is the key. In camp, a handful of ice on the stung area eases pain, too. Bee venom is acidic, so a paste of baking soda and water neutralizes its sting. A wasp's venom is alkaline, so an application of an acid (vinegar, lemon juice) does the trick. There are also several plants whose juices can alleviate some stinging (see the section about natural remedies later in this chapter).

In the case of stinging insects, some leave the stinger in the wound (bees, for instance) while others (wasps, scorpions) keep the stinger to strike again. In the case of the bee, it's important to carefully scrape the area of the sting with a narrow straight edge to remove the sting sac of the bee from the wound. Grabbing the sac with your fingers has a tendency to squeeze even more of the painful venom into the wound. Wasp and hornets can sting their victim several times. There are several medical applications you can use to lessen the pain or itch of a sting.

Bleeding

Direct pressure is the best method for stopping bleeding. The two main exceptions to this rule are neck wounds, where direct pressure can compromise the airway (instead of pressure, pinch the wound shut), or severe head injuries, where there is a danger of pressing skull fragments into the brain (use a bulky dressing and gentle pressure to help absorb the blood).

Survival Tip: **Wound Irrigation**

No syringe to irrigate the wound? Get a small plastic bag, sterilize it with boiling water or other sterilizing agents and fill it about two-thirds full with clean, disinfected water. When you are ready to irrigate the wound, seal the bag and puncture a lower corner of the water-filled sack with a pin or other small point to create a solid, steady flow of water. Direct the water to the wound and flush the wound accordingly.

Especially with children, wound irrigation is an important treatment component to reduce the presence of bacteria, which can lead to serious infections.

One of the first steps in preparing a wound for a dressing is to irrigate the wound to flush out any foreign particles or other remnants that might encourage infection. Most kits come with an irrigation syringe for this purpose. Use disinfected water and flush the wound from above making sure the solution and debris are washed from the wound.

Wounds should be closed together before dressing if possible. Butterfly closures work well in pulling pieces of skin together. Some first aid kits include "super" glue that can be used to actually glue the edges of skin back together. The dressing should completely cover the wound. It should be

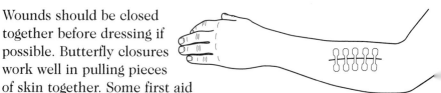

sterile, porous and easy to apply, and it should not stick to the wound.

Once the dressing is applied and the area cleaned, a bandage covering the area can be applied. The bandage should keep the area clean and dry. Sometimes it is best to add new dressing instead of replacing old ones in the field. A bandage can be used as long as it remains clean and dry and continues to protect and support the wound.

***

Survival Tip: Tourniquet

I grew up learning, wrongly, to never use a tourniquet except in life-threatening situations and that once it was in place, never remove it. A better course of action is to use the tourniquet only if there is a tremendous amount of bleeding that cannot be stopped by direct pressure alone.

The proper material for a tourniquet is a band of cloth or other material at least 2 to 4 inches (5 to 10 cm) wide. It is critical that the tourniquet be applied close to the wound but on the heart (upper) side of the elbow or knee joint—never below it, even for a hand or foot injury. The tourniquet should be secured only to the point where the flow of blood stops and then should be loosened and checked in about 10 minutes to see if the blood has formed a clot.

The tourniquet can be retightened if needed but should never be left on any longer than is absolutely necessary.

***

Blisters

The common, annoying blister is an indication that something isn't fitting correctly, so make that your first priority. A thin, inner pair of socks over a heavier, outer layer sometimes helps, as long as there are no folds or other uneven areas prone to cause irritation on the skin. Moleskin can be applied to reduce friction in an area. It is not unanimous, but some suggest using a sterile pin to puncture the base of a cleaned, unbroken blister and then treating the area like a wound.

Broken Bones

Breaks can be very painful and can cause other problems such as infection and bleeding. There are techniques for applying splints to almost every part of the body, including traction splits for leg injuries. Most important, the

splint must immobilize the injury above and below the break and support it in a natural position. Dislocations, multiple breaks or compound fractures must be dealt with directly. A splint holds the bones in place while preventing movement of the limbs associated with the break, so the material used in the splint must cushion the injury but be stout enough to immobilize the injury. Besides those splints that come with some kits (the SAM Splint is a very versatile, flexible splint, available in a variety of lengths and widths), consider layers of newspaper, rolled magazines, even pieces of bark from certain trees.

Most of the better medical/first aid kits include a step-by-step booklet with instruction on how to deal with broken bones—be prepared, do your homework, take a class.

Burns

Burns have got to be one of the most painful of injuries. The first treatment for a burn is, of course, to remove the source of the heat. Sometimes the burning continues, so water should be used to stop the burning and to cool the wound. The extent of burns over a human body can be assessed in the field using formulas that accurately estimate the percentage of body area affected by burns.

This can be vital information to transmit to responders over the radio if you are fortunate to have that luxury.

Treatment for burns includes washing the area in slightly warm water and soap, removing all loose skin, debris and popped blisters (never pop closed burn blisters), and covering the area with an ointment dressing. Apply loose coverings and, unless evacuation is immediate, remove and change dressings very carefully. Do not use ice to pack a burn.

Survival Tip: **Burn Help**

If you have no ointment or other burn treatment, allow the burn to scab over. Ibuprofen is one of the best painkillers for burns. If skin has been lost, help keep the victim hydrated by offering plenty of water. Burns around the neck and mouth area may restrict the airway. Always make sure, with any face and neck injury, that the airway is clear.

Dental Problems

Losing a filling or experiencing a throbbing cavity can ruin the best of camping trips and add to the stress of survival situations. Filling the cavity with wax, sugarless gum or treatments from the first aid kit, such as 3M's Cavit, or a few drops of oil of cloves can ease the pain.

If a tooth is knocked out, it can be gently seeded back into the jaw, or wrapped and kept cool for replacement later. Aspirin can be used if applied against exposed pulp in a tooth cavity. Never apply aspirin where it will become exposed to the gums, as the acid will burn the gums. Swallow the aspirin instead.

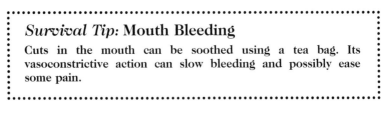

Survival Tip: **Mouth Bleeding**

Cuts in the mouth can be soothed using a tea bag. Its vasoconstrictive action can slow bleeding and possibly ease some pain.

Dehydration
See Chapter 5 for a complete discussion.

Frostbite

Degrees of frostbite injuries can be classified in
at least two ways. The most common method,
as described in *Medicine for the Outdoors* by
Paul S. Auerbach, M.D., compares the appear-
ance and severity of frostbite to a burn by
assigning degree ratings: numbness and redness
(first degree), superficial blistering (second
degree), deep blistering (third degree) and
extremely deep, sometimes including bone
(fourth degree).

In Buck Tilton's *Backcountry First Aid*, frostbite is classified as either "partial-thickness"
frostbite or "full-thickness" frostbite. With the partial
variety, the frostbitten skin is pale and numb but still
pliable. Treatment includes warming the frostbitten area
with another warm body part (warm hand to the area, or,
in the case of a frostbitten hand, to a warm stomach or
armpit). Do not rub the affected area and do not try to
rewarm by placing the affected area too close to an
intense heat source or open flame. Give Ibuprofen and
encourage the victim to drink lots of water.

Full-thickness frostbite means the frozen area is pale,
numb and hard. The best treatment is to rewarm the
affected area as quickly as possible in water between 104
and 108°F (40 and 42°C). The thawing of frozen flesh is
excruciatingly painful. Ibuprofen to the rescue again!

Once the affected area is thawed (usually about 30
minutes), the afflicted area should not be covered so
tightly that any material or fabric actually touches the
area.

Warning: Do not thaw a frozen, frostbitten area if there is any chance it might refreeze. If evacuation requires exposing the frostbitten area to freezing temperatures again, do not attempt to thaw the area. Keeping the part frozen is most critical. "Frost nip" is another cold-weather term that refers to ice crystals that form on the surface of the skin but do not freeze the skin or underlying layers. A little localized warming is usually sufficient to melt the ice crystals.

Heat Exhaustion

If you work too hard, too long, get too dehydrated and become exhausted from the heat, you are suffering from heat exhaustion. Overextending yourself on a hot day is naturally tiring and exhaustive. Victims tend to be very young or very old, usually overweight and dehydrated. Humidity is usually high, and the victim is unaccustomed to heat. Victims can feel nauseous and dizzy and appear sweaty and pale. The cure is usually straightforward: Cool the victim, have the person rest and rehydrate him or her. Do not give a victim of heat exhaustion a salt tablet; rather, add just a pinch of salt to about a quart (liter) of water. To rapidly cool a victim, wet the person and fan his or her body to generate a cooling effect. Recovery is usually complete and without side effects.

Heat Stroke

If the body's core temperature gets too hot (above 105°F/ 40.5°C) the brain can heat up, creating a life-threatening emergency that must be dealt with immediately. A victim suffering from heat stroke will be disoriented, have an increased heart rate, have faster breathing and complain of headaches. Significant and unusual personality changes may occur as well.

Heat-stroke victims need to be cooled down immediately. Heat-retaining clothing should be removed and the victim wetted thoroughly to begin the cooling process. Direct cooling to the head and neck of the victim. Cold packs on the palms of hands, soles of the feet, groin, armpits, neck and head can speed the cooling process. Once cooled, rubbing the extremities aids in getting that coolness to the inner core.

Even if victims appear recovered, a doctor should be consulted as soon as possible.

Hyponatremia

Long-distance runners and other athletes probably already know about hyponatremia, a state of low levels of sodium in the blood. The problem arises from drinking too much water that is deficient in needed salts and electrolytes. Because the symptoms are similar to dehydration, the solution would seem to be to give the victim more water. However, the difference between the two is that in dehydration victims, the urine is colored (usually yellow), while the hyponatremia victim's urine is clear, and the victim feels properly hydrated. The treatment for hyponatremia is to get the victim to rest and prevent them from drinking water. Gradually offer the victim salty foods.

Survival Tip: **Monitor Others**

A quick way to assess members of your party for the beginning signs of hypothermia is to monitor their actions without them knowing your concern. For example, if you are hiking, you can fall behind a suspected hypothermia victim to observe a slight meandering or reduction of coordination. This test can be used to detect the onset of dehydration, too—similar symptoms begin as the body responds to lack of water.

Hypothermia

The number-one killer in survival situations demands mention again in this book. Recognizing the signs of hypothermia is an important second step in treatment.

The first step is, of course, to prepare with proper clothing and shelter to ward off hypothermia in the first place.

Some early signs include loss of coordination, loss of fine motor skills, uncontrollable shivering and then a stop to the shivering.

First aid for a hypothermia victim is as follows:
1. Check for an open airway and vital signs. Pulse and breathing may be weak. Start CPR immediately if either is missing.
2. Prevent further heat loss; carefully move the victim to shelter and warmth.
3. Gently remove all wet/cold clothing—cut it away if you must.
4. Wrap the victim in blankets, a sleeping bag or other warm covering and place warm water bottles inside the wrap, around the victim's neck, groin and sides of chest (you are trying to rewarm the body core).
5. Transport the victim to a hospital as soon as possible.

Survival Tip: **Drowning**

In the case of a capsized boat, several methods are often suggested to help victims keep from drowning. One method is called "drown proofing" and involves staying afloat in the water, with head down, and raising your head every 10 or 15 seconds for air. It is designed to save energy. Beware: Drown proofing requires that the head be underwater, which results in a tremendous amount of heat loss. Drown proofing in cold water reduces survival rates by about 50 percent!

Instead, use the Heat Escape Lessening Posture (HELP). Keep your head up, knees pulled up to your chest and arms hugging your knees. Wearing a personal floating device/life jacket can prohibit proper form in the HELP position, so you may have to modify your form—as long as your head is above water.

The "huddle" is a group hug method where three people float and tread water vertically while facing each other and interlocking their arms. A child or adult can be placed in the center of this group and individual members of the huddle can rotate into the center to keep warm.

If you spend any time outdoors, even in temperate climates in the summer, learn about hypothermia. It is critical to know what to do, as well as what not to do to treat hypothermia victims:

1. Do not place an unconscious victim in a bathtub.
2. Do not give the victim anything to drink, including hot liquids and especially alcohol.
3. Do not rub the victim's skin; do not rub it with snow!

Infection

A reddening, tenderness or swelling of the skin is a sign of infection. The creation of pus in the wound or red streaks just under the skin are other telltale signs that infection has set in. Soaking the wound in very hot water and redressing is one treatment against infection. Packing the wound with sterile gauze can help the wound drain.

No improvement in a serious wound or a victim's condition, serious infection from animal bites or infections to the head and face area all require immediate evacuation.

Rabies

The only reason I bring up rabies is the possibility that someone may decide to set one of the many trap contraptions illustrated in some military survival manuals. A rabid animal may be more approachable, and therefore seemingly easier to catch or trap.

If bitten by a wild creature, wash the wound immediately and very aggressively, and then keep the wound open to allow for drainage.

Treatment for rabies today is much less painful than in years gone by. The shots, like those for diabetes, are administered just under the skin, as opposed to those long spike-like needles pushed deep into stomach muscles in the past.

Snakebite

The first treatment is prevention. Avoid hiding places in snake country and be careful to avoid stepping onto or grabbing too closely to areas where snakes (cold-blooded reptiles) may be resting in the shade. Treatments for most snakebites in temperate areas include removing any restrictive clothing, using an extractor to suck out as much venom as possible, supporting the limb in a sling to keep it stationary and keeping the wound at the same level as the heart.

Do not use cold packs or ice on snakebites. Most snake venoms have antidotes available. Snakebites in tropical countries are another, much more serious matter because of the number of poisonous species, the remoteness of areas and the availability (or even existence) of a proper antidote.

Sprains and Strains

Before treating these musculoskeletal injuries, it is helpful to know the difference between them. A sprain is an injury to a ligament, those bands that hold one bone to another. A strain is an overstretched muscle or tendon. A strained area can be used up to the point where it generates pain—at which point, simply stop.

RICE is an acronym that represents the four components to treating sprains and strains:

➤ Rest

➤ Ice

➤ Compression

➤ Elevation

It comes in handy for remembering how to treat these ailments. Before applying the RICE treatment, check to make sure the joint is not broken (can it be moved, used?). If it's not broken, begin. Otherwise you may need to apply a splint first. If you are not sure whether it is a sprain/strain or break, use a splint, just in case.

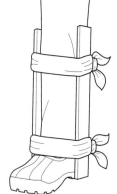

The victim should not use the sprained or strained joint during the RICE treatment. Rather, the victim should sit or lie down (rest), taking weight off the sprain/strain. Ice should then be applied— not directly, but first contained in a piece of material, something to insulate the injury from direct contact with the ice. In lieu of ice, you can use cold water absorbed into a cloth, sponge or suitable carrier (moss soaked in a cold stream, for example). Compression can be achieved by applying an elastic wrap. Finally, elevate the injured area. After about a half hour of this treatment, the wrap and ice can be removed and the injured area allowed to warm up for about 10 to 15 minutes before attempting to use it.

***

Survival Tip: Makeshift Splint

A triangle bandage, if large enough, can be used to tie a walking splint around injured ankles. The bandage serves as a compression wrap and a modest retainer to keep the ankle from moving too far or fast.

***

Vision Problems

Small, loose particles can be flushed from the eye using an irrigation syringe or makeshift flushers. A large object, particularly one that may be imbedded in the eye, should be protected from being bumped, and the victim evacuated. There are special ointments that can be applied directly to the eye.

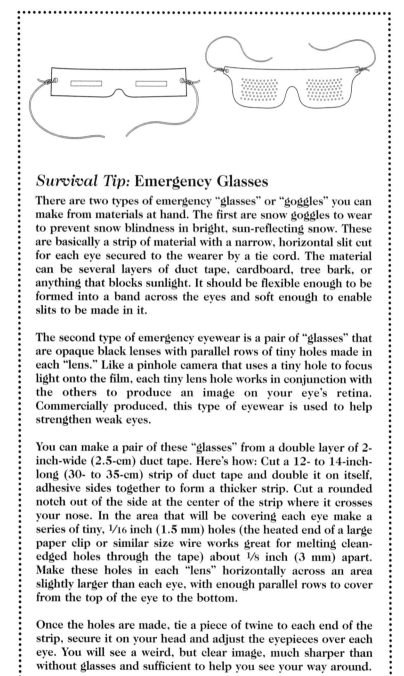

Survival Tip: Emergency Glasses

There are two types of emergency "glasses" or "goggles" you can make from materials at hand. The first are snow goggles to wear to prevent snow blindness in bright, sun-reflecting snow. These are basically a strip of material with a narrow, horizontal slit cut for each eye secured to the wearer by a tie cord. The material can be several layers of duct tape, cardboard, tree bark, or anything that blocks sunlight. It should be flexible enough to be formed into a band across the eyes and soft enough to enable slits to be made in it.

The second type of emergency eyewear is a pair of "glasses" that are opaque black lenses with parallel rows of tiny holes made in each "lens." Like a pinhole camera that uses a tiny hole to focus light onto the film, each tiny lens hole works in conjunction with the others to produce an image on your eye's retina. Commercially produced, this type of eyewear is used to help strengthen weak eyes.

You can make a pair of these "glasses" from a double layer of 2-inch-wide (2.5-cm) duct tape. Here's how: Cut a 12- to 14-inch-long (30- to 35-cm) strip of duct tape and double it on itself, adhesive sides together to form a thicker strip. Cut a rounded notch out of the side at the center of the strip where it crosses your nose. In the area that will be covering each eye make a series of tiny, 1/16 inch (1.5 mm) holes (the heated end of a large paper clip or similar size wire works great for melting clean-edged holes through the tape) about 1/8 inch (3 mm) apart. Make these holes in each "lens" horizontally across an area slightly larger than each eye, with enough parallel rows to cover from the top of the eye to the bottom.

Once the holes are made, tie a piece of twine to each end of the strip, secure it on your head and adjust the eyepieces over each eye. You will see a weird, but clear image, much sharper than without glasses and sufficient to help you see your way around.

Bright snow can lead to snow blindness (actually, sun-burned eyes), which creates a gritty, irritating feeling in the victim's eyes. The eye should be rinsed with cold, clean water and specific antibiotic eye ointments can be applied. Prevent snow blindness by wearing sunglasses with UV-blocking lenses.

Wounds
The skin can be wounded in several ways:

➤ It can be bruised but not penetrated. A big danger with a bruise is that the incident may have also damaged underlying organs or caused internal bleeding.

➤ An avulsion is when a large flap of skin is ripped open. The flap should be held open and the underlying area thoroughly irrigated. The flap should then be put back, dressed and bandaged.

➤ A laceration is a jagged cut in the skin—a superficial cut or a deep, penetrating slice into and sometimes completely through the layers of skin. Cleaning the wound, closing the wound, applying a dressing and then applying bandages is the basic treatment for a laceration.

➤ A puncture wound is one in which the skin is impaled or otherwise penetrated. The object, unless loose, should be left in place and the dressing/bandage applied around it, securing it all until treatment.

➤ Abrasions or scrapes are surface wounds that need to be cleaned thoroughly. Some medical kits include a special scrub brush to literally scrub the debris from the wound. If that sounds like it could really hurt, you are right! Some kits offer a special sponge for scrubbing; in lieu of either, a clump of sterile gauze could be used. After scrubbing, irrigate the wound, apply a dressing and then cover it with a bandage.

FIRST AID TIPS FOR CHILDREN

Depending on their age, many body functions are not fully developed in children to the point that those functions are ready to perform in stressful situations. A child's exterior body may be more developed than the internal systems growing to support or protect him or her.

Dehydration

Use oral rehydration solutions (ORS) to replace lost salts and add a little energy for children suffering from dehydration caused by any of the usual culprits (diarrhea, vomiting, heat). Use 1 teaspoon (5 ml) of sugar and a pinch of salt to 1 quart (1 l) of water if you don't have a commercial ORS product. Avoid salt tablets as they are too concentrated.

Diarrhea

As children suffer from diarrhea they, like adults, may become dehydrated—but at a faster rate. Dark yellow urine is a sign of dehydration. Children may also have a loss of appetite, suffer from headaches and have other symptoms that might suggest flu.

Diarrhea medicines are available and can help. Infants should be fed rice cereal, applesauce or bananas; older children should eat bland foods such as dry toast, plain crackers, even chicken broth.

Heat Exhaustion

Allow children more time to acclimate to changes in heat to which they are unaccustomed. Encourage them to drink more water than they feel they need. Adding flavorings can encourage the consumption of water.

Poisonous Plants

Of all the poisonous plants in nature, poison ivy has to rank as not only one of the most common, but also the most multiformed of the group. It can be a simple ground-covering plant, a modest vine climbing up a tree trunk or a bush with 1-inch-thick (2.5-cm) branches—all bearing the telltale three-lobed, compound-leaf characteristic of this annoying plant.

Learn which plants are poisonous plants (poison ivy, poison oak, poison sumac, stinging nettles) and teach your children how to identify them. Suspected exposed skin should be cleaned with soap and water immediately. Any clothing that might have come in contact with the poison ivy/oak/sumac should be washed, too. Hydrocortisone cream or calamine lotions will ease the symptoms, and time will heal the affected area.

In the case of ingested poisons of most kinds, give the child a couple of cups of water and then induce vomiting. Warning: Do not induce vomiting if the suspected poison is corrosive or if the victim is having a seizure, is unconscious or has ingested petroleum products.

> ### Survival Tip: Jellyfish
> A maritime "cure" for attacks by jellyfish is to use human urine to wash off and deactivate the nematocysts. In a pinch, it works!

Poisonous Marine Life

There are many threats of poison in the ocean, most of which are spines and other stingers on creatures children may be tempted to play with on a beach or come in contact with in the water. In the case of spines, removing them and soaking the affected area in hot water for about an hour or so can relieve the pain and reduce the chances of infection. In the case of a jellyfish sting, use saltwater to rinse off the affected area and use a firm straight edge (such as the back of a knife) to scrape the area in a downward direction only to remove the "stingers." Do not use fresh water. A soak or wash with vinegar or alcohol

171

can help deactivate the toxins as well.

Stings and Bites

Lower concentrations of DEET in insect repellents are recommended for children. For insect bites that have been scratched into open wounds, clean the bite area and cover with a bandage. Hydrocortisone cream can be applied to relieve itching from more established bites.

> *Survival Tip:* **Itching**
>
> A paste made of baking soda or commercial meat tenderizer can be applied to most insect bites to relieve itching. (Other natural remedies are cited later in this chapter.)

Sunburn

Too much sun as a youth can affect an adult much later in life. Children burn more easily than do adults and should be clothed to protect them from the harmful UV rays of the sun. This includes long-sleeve shirts and pants and hats with adequate visors. Sunscreens with higher sun protection factor (SPF) numbers should be used and considered less effective than a number might indicate (so choose slightly higher). On infants, test a small area of skin for any reactions to SPF lotions. Never use baby oil in the sun because it does not contain any sunscreen.

Sunburn treatment includes putting cool compresses on sunburned areas, applying moisturizing lotions and drinking lots of water. Acetaminophen can relieve pain.

TYPES OF FIRST AID KITS

A critical part of your medical kit should be any required medicines for members of your party. Special medicines and doses for children should be included as well (chewable medicines, perhaps). Equally important is to list the dosages on the outside of each medication so someone

172

unfamiliar with a person's particular needs can administer the medications.

Do your homework when purchasing a medical/first aid kit. Some kits claim to include more than 300 items only to load the kit down with 200 wound closure strips or adhesive bandages and little else of consequence. Other kits contain an incredible inventory of supplies including emergency blankets and water pouches.

It is important to find a kit that will best serve your group's anticipated needs. Specific medications and pre-scription drugs should be added as needed, as well as items you think are important but not included in a particular kit. Remember, this is the kit you intend to have with you at all times, at least at a base camp. The more weighty and cumbersome it is, the less likely you may be to bring it or more likely you will leave it in the car at the start of a 20-mile (32-km) cross-country hike.

Leading producers of backcountry/wilderness kits offer several different configurations to help the consumer tar-get specific activities, needs and group sizes. There are kits for the mountain biker, day-tripper and multisportster—right up to the luggage-size shipboard units that rival a M.A.S.H. unit. Most kits are organized into units of need, either gear specific or medication/treatment specific.

Kits usually contain items for four general types of treatments:

➤ **Wound management,** which includes irrigation tools, iodine, antibiotic ointment, wound closure strips, tincture of Benzoin.

➤ **Infection,** which includes sanitary wipes and exam gloves.

➤ **Bandages,** which includes a variety of adhesive wound closures and bandages in various sizes and quantities, knuckle bandages, a variety of gauze patch and pads, elastic bandages and wraps, various sterile dressings.

➤ **Medications,** which are over-the-counter treatments. Make sure you understand which medications are used for which ailments. Typically included in this inventory are antihistamines for respiratory allergy and cold symptoms; aspirin; ORS and electrolyte replacements; hydrocortisone for relief from poisonous plants, Ibuprofen for headaches, pain, toothache, menstrual cramps, diarrhea, sting relief.

Other suggested items are tweezers, matches, safety pins (an extremely versatile item) and a small compass.

Kit Contents

Below is an inventory of the contents of a typical field medical kit. It is a compilation of items found in several of the leading kits on the market today. Because manufacturers offer different kits for different activities and in different sizes, the type and number of actual items will vary among the kits within a manufacturer's product line as well as among manufacturers. An alternative to a prepacked kit is to go to a medical supply outlet and purchase these items separately—although you may not find that as economical as these kits. For refilling or expanding a kit to cover specific anticipated needs, such supply stores should stock those items not available at your drug store (and generic brands are cheaper, anyway).

Qty.	Item
1	First aid booklet, information sheet or flashcards with treatments listed
4–6	Rolls of adhesive tape (½" x 10 yd/12 mm x 9 m)
1–2	Large sterile gauze dressings (3 x 3"/7.6 x 7.6 cm, 4 x 4"/10 x 10 cm)
4–6	Gauze bandages or 2" x 4 yd (5 cm x 3.6 m) roll

1	Fabric adhesive bandage (1 x 3"/2.5 x 7.6 cm)
1–2	Trauma pad (5 x 9"/12.7 x 22.8 cm)
1–2	Non-adhesive pad (2 x 3"/5 x 7.6 cm or 3 x 4"/7.6 x 10 cm)
4–5	Moleskin pads (various sizes)
2–4	Sterile wound closures (sometimes called butterfly bandages)
2–4	Knuckle bandages
2–4	Ibuprofen (Motrin, Advil) for pain relief from headache, cold, minor muscle/joint discomfort; suggested for those allergic to aspirin.
1–2	Acetaminophen (Tylenol) for pain relief from headache, colds, toothache, burns, or for fever reduction
2–4	Antihistamine (diphenhydramine) for treatment of allergic symptoms (respiratory, anaphylaxis), relief of itching from allergic skin reactions, mild sedative
1–2	Aspirin for inflammation and fever
1	Antibiotic ointment to prevent infection, minor relief from itching
1	Tincture of benzoin: increases holding power of adhesive bandages.
1	Providone iodine pad
1	Sting relief pad or After Bite wipe (relief of insect bites)
1 pair	Examination gloves
1	Utility scissors
1	EMT scissors
1	Sterile scalpel blade
2–4	Safety pins
1	SAM Splint
2–4	Elastic bandage with closure
1	Tongue depressor
1	Sterile eye patch
1	Thermometer (digital)
1	Snake bite extractor

Other items vary by specific focus of kit (backpacking, kayaking, etc.) and may contain different quantities of these items. Additional items that come standard in kits include antiseptic wipes, green soap and sponge, hard sugar candies, syringe irrigator, nasal spray, super glue, triangular bandages, duct tape and pencil/paper.

MEDICINAL PLANT REMEDIES

Long before drug stores and traveling snake-oil salesmen, humans used plants for their medicinal value. Much of the success of finding healing plants was trial and error, based upon years of observation and chance. If a plant had features that resembled the human head, that part was gathered and used to treat head ailments. Some worked, some did not. Some healing plants and other natural remedies have even worked their way into mainstream treatments for what ails us. As a survival-savvy adventurer, knowing at least a few of the basic plants and makeshift remedies may give you the edge to help a victim survive.

You may also observe that most of medicinal plants also appear on edible plant lists. Like wild edibles, if you don't know what something is, don't use it. Get a good plant identification book and research the topic of medicinal herbs and plants. Such references can be studied in the field during all seasons to help you better learn and identify the plants you are most likely to consider in a survival situation. Many plant identification books include a section on each plant's other attributes, including medicinal use.

A great source of information on North American plants with specific medicinal and food value is Alaska's Wilderness Medicines: Healthful Plants of the Far North, by Eleanor G. Viereck. Don't let the title fool you; it lists plants that are quite common across the United States and Canada.

Survival Tip: **Plant Names**

Look up the Latin name of a plant to learn if the second part of the name is *officinale*, as in *Taraxacum officinale*, the Latin name for the common dandelion (an edible and medicinal plant). This method of naming plants was used to indicate that a plant was, at one time, an official remedy for several ailments.

Here is a partial list of the more common and plentiful plants in nature's medicine chest:

➤ **Alder:** Boiled bark tea used to rid stomach of gas, lower high fever. Leaves have been used to cure inflammation of the feet.

➤ **Birch:** Tea from leaves used to treat gout, rheumatism. The bark of the sweet birch contains salicylic acid—aspirin! A decoction (an infusion made in boiling water) of bark can be used to bathe skin eruptions.

➤ **Chickweed:** Used to treat infections and inflammations, burns, skin diseases and more. It is edible, raw or cooked, too.

➤ **Dandelion:** Mild detergent, laxative and diuretic. A tasty, edible substitute for spinach.

➤ **Fireweed:** Tea from leaves used to treat stomachaches.

➤ **Highbush cranberry:** A cup of tea made from a handful of bark shavings is a treatment to relax muscles and menstrual cramps. A decoction from leaves aids a sore throat.

➤ **Juniper:** Berries are chewed raw or steeped into a tea to stimulate the genitourinary tract, also to stimulate the brain, to increase heat and for rheumatic pains.

➤ **Labrador:** Leaves used to make a tea to treat colds; very tasty, it can be added to other teas. High in ascorbic acid (vitamin C).

➤ **Lowbush cranberry:** Chew berries to treat a sore throat, upset stomach. Heat the berries and use as a hot pack for headaches, swelling and sore throats.

➤ **Plantain:** Pound leaves into a paste to help check bleeding. Tea made from leaves can be applied to skin irritations and diseases. Mashed green plantain can also be applied to insect bites. Plantain has myriad uses as both a medicinal and edible plant. It is high in vitamin A and C, and can be used in green salads or as a cooked vegetable.

➤ **Shepherd's purse:** Used externally as a poultice (soft, heated mass combined in a porous cloth and applied to problem area) on wounds to stop bleeding (high in vitamin K).

➤ **Sphagnum moss:** A soft, acidic plant that absorbs moisture better than a sponge, used for dressing of wounds. One source says sphagnum moss is high in iodine.

➤ **Spruce:** Its pitch is used to dress wounds and as a medication for cuts and scratches. It prevents infection.

➤ **Uva-ursi:** Also called kinnikinnick or bearberry, the tea from its leaves is used as treatment for relieving kidney and bladder problems. When leaves are smoked as a tobacco, it is said to alleviate headaches.

➤ **Willow:** An ancient source of aspirin, an infusion of willow bark aids in treatment of pain, fever and other ailments. A mash made from chewed leaves and placed on a bee sting will keep it from swelling.

➤ **Yarrow:** Its antiseptic properties are effective when used to pack wounds. Also its leaves are used to treat earaches and toothaches.

The key to first aid in a survival situation is to identify the injury, determine what has to be done to treat the injury (stop bleeding, immobilize a part, reduce swelling, etc.) and then determine what you can use to accomplish that treatment. You may not have a kit or instructions available to you. You may have to pack a bleeding lower arm wound with sphagnum moss and secure it with a bandage made from strips of a T-shirt that is then secured to the victim's chest with a safety pin. You may want to give the victim a dose of aspirin, too. Knowing what to do, coupled with the right resources, can make all the difference—when you think like a survivor.

Components of a Survival Kit

Anticipating what particular tools you might need in a survival situation is like predicting what clothes you'll need for a destination you know nothing about. You can bring general gear that covers a range of conditions, but specific needs will have to be augmented with what's at hand.

Such is the case in survival situations when you have no forewarning about conditions, location, circumstances or makeup of the victim or victims. Still, having basic tools and, more importantly, knowing how to use them and how to adapt tools as needed, will be strong factors in your favor, no matter what survival situation you find yourself in.

Anyone who teaches survival and talks about kits will tell you the same thing: "If you don't actually carry it with you, you do *not* have a survival kit!" Knowing this, carrying only essential gear—gear that is not too bulky, cumbersome or weighty— becomes critical.

Also, since space is at a premium, choose individual tools that can perform multiple tasks, instead of taking several single-purpose items.

When you consider that most survival kits sold commercially come in a metal container not much bigger than a large can of tuna, and even homemade kits weigh less than 5 pounds (2.2 kg), you can understand the importance of concise, compacted and multipurpose survival gear.

A good survival kit should fit on your belt or in a pocket of some item you are wearing, and be with you *at all times*. Think "socks," "underwear," "survival kit" if it helps drive that point home!

CONTENTS

I began survival training in the Boy Scouts, but it wasn't until I took several classes from Dave Watkins in Alaska that I truly began to feel a sense for it, a true responsibility to self and others to learn and practice what I could to stay proficient and current in the areas of survival know-how. Dave and his associates put together their own survival kits. I still use a Watkins survival kit today, although I have expanded on some of the gear. Here are the components of the kit and the rationale for their inclusion in some cases:

➤ Aluminum container, with lid and metal clasps—sized to carry gear, yet small enough to fit in a pocket. Metal container can be used for collecting and boiling water (some kits have plastic clasps which will melt from heat) and cooking. Reflective surface is a signaling mirror. Survival hints are written on inside of lid (seven steps, water treatment, ground/air signals, etc.).

➤ 2 x 3" (5 x 7.6 cm) signal mirror—on lanyard, with instructions for use on back. Personally, I'd augment this with one more, larger 3 x 5" mirror, for self-inspection, back signaling and larger direct-signaling surface.

➤ Two 3" (7.6 cm) wax-coated fire sticks—with strike-anywhere match heads imbedded in one end. (These can deteriorate over time, so inspect and replace as needed). Also consider all-weather waterproof matches or butane lighter).

➤ Magnesium bar/striker kit—small spark-generating kit; can be placed on lanyard with signal mirror and worn around neck, too.

➤ Sewing kit—with felt patch, three safety pins and two needles. In addition, wrap this kit with several feet (1 m) of extra-strong thread and dental floss. Safety pins have myriad uses, from holding a sling to a shirt to fish hooks.

➤ ½ fluid ounce (15 ml) Provodine iodine. Besides its anti-septic qualities, use 8 drops per quart (liter) to purify water.

➤ Fishing kit—literally hook, line and sinkers. The stout nylon fishing line can be used for lashing, repairing cloth items and other binding needs. Hooks and swivels could be used to secure items together when zippers break.

➤ Two 18" (46 cm) sections of snare wire (eyelet at one end)—I don't think many of us will have the know-how to properly set a snare, in the right place, to catch enough game to be worth the effort. Nevertheless, this wire can be used to bind, repair, etc. With a large enough battery source, it could be heated to start a fire, too.

➤ First aid kit—consists mostly of various-size adhesive strips to treat the most common injuries (skin wounds). Adding packets of medicines for headache, sore throat, sinuses and upset stomach from a larger first aid kit will round out this kit. I would add a few 4 x 4" (10 x 10 cm) sterile gauze pads, too.

➤ 10' (3 m) of ⅛"-diameter (0.3-cm) nylon cord—parachute cord is best. This can be used for lashing, creating handles or fastening foot-, hand- and headwear from makeshift materials.

➤ Packets of tea, soup, drink flavoring—a variety to suit your tastes and add flavoring to treated water.

➤ Small candle—ideal for starting a fire. Also, the wax can seal small leaks, and a ball of it can be pressed into a lost cavity filling for temporary dental first aid.

➤ Sunscreen/lip balm—personally I don't find this to be an essential item. I'd rather use the space for a small roll of duct tape or more matches.

These items represent what's commonly found in many kits through the outdoor retail shelves. To further personalize a kit, I would add the following items:

➤ 1 space blanket or emergency tube tent.

➤ 6 cotton balls saturated with petroleum jelly (for starting fires).

➤ 1 collapsible quart (liter) or gallon (3.8 l) water container with lid/closure spout.

➤ 1 pea-less signal whistle—I'd wear one, too. This is an extra whistle.

➤ 2 heavy-duty trash bags—extra stout, large enough to use as clothing or shelter. Bright colors to attract attention, black for snow use.

➤ 1 small flashlight (LED); extra battery (batteries, like matches, can be stuffed in numerous places throughout gear to be used regularly).

➤ 1 small bottle hot spice sauce (Tabasco). If it works for the Coast Guard...

➤ 1–2 nutrition/candy bars. As in any kit with perishables, check yours before and after every outing. Moisture is a big destroyer of quality and usefulness.

Additional tips: I like to add extra nylon cord to my kits by wrapping several lengths around handles or sheaths—it's out of the way and is stored for easy access. Also, all these items should be in brightly colored containers and/or covered with bright colors for easy sighting if dropped. Larger items that can be waved overhead or visible for a long distance should also be brightly colored. Stuff bags, hats, outer leggings, your tent fly and windbreaker can all be used as emergency flag signals, and the bright colors only help.

Duct tape is invaluable for repairs and even to hold bandages and splints in place. Use bright colors instead of ductwork gray for higher visibility. Wrap several layers around gear to be pulled off and used as necessary.

A smaller knife and a sharpening tool can be included in your kit. A larger utility knife with the shank into the handle should be carried on your belt or around your neck. It, too, is a mini-survival kit that is only good if you carry it with you.

Appendix II

Lost on the Moon Test
(Revisited)

In Chapter 3 you were asked to complete this test but not look up the correct order until you had taken the test again after reading the entire book. It's now time to take the test again. Check your later test answers against your first answers and compare them to the correct order on the next page. Even if you get them right both times, it helps to reinforce the need to think through and prepare for all sorts of situations.

Lost on the Moon Test

Your spaceship has just crash-landed on the moon. You were scheduled to rendezvous with a mother ship 200 miles away (320 km) on the moon's lighted surface, but the rough landing has ruined your ship and destroyed all the equipment on board, except for the 15 items listed below.

Your crew's survival depends on reaching the mother ship, so you must choose the most critical items available for the 200-mile (320-km) moon trek. Your task is to rank the items in terms of their importance for survival.

Place number one by the most important item, number two by the second most important item, and so on through number fifteen, the least important item:

_____ Box of matches
_____ 50 feet (15 m) of nylon rope
_____ Two .45 caliber pistols
_____ Self-inflating life raft
_____ Five gallons (19 l) of water
_____ First aid kit (containing injection needles)
_____ Solar-powered FM receiver-transmitter
_____ Stellar map (of the moon's constellation)
_____ Two 100-pound (45-kg) tanks of oxygen
_____ Solar-powered portable heating unit

_____ Food concentrate
_____ Parachute silk
_____ One case of dehydrated milk
_____ Magnetic compass
_____ Signal flares

Lost on the Moon Test Answers

Here are the answers, in order of priority:
1. Two 100-pound (45-kg) tanks of oxygen—most pressing survival need.
2. Five gallons (19 l) of water—replacement for tremendous liquid loss on lighted side.
3. Stellar map of moon's constellations—primary means of navigation.
4. Food concentrate—efficient means of supplying energy.
5. Solar-powered FM receiver-transmitter—for communication with mother ship (but FM requires line-of-sight and short ranges).
6. 50 feet (15 m) of nylon rope—useful in scaling cliffs, tying injured together.
7. First aid kit (injection needles)—needles for vitamins, medicines, etc. (Will fit special aperture in NASA. Free point, how were you to know?)
8. Parachute silk—protection from sun's rays.
9. Self-inflating life raft—CO_2 bottle in military raft may be useful for propulsion.
10. Signal flares—distress signal when mother ship is sighted.
11. Two .45 caliber pistols—possible means of self-propulsion.
12. One case of dehydrated milk—bulkier duplication of food concentrate.
13. Solar-powered portable heating unit—not needed unless on dark side of moon.
14. Magnet compass—magnetic field on moon is not polarized; worthless.
15. Box of matches—no oxygen on moon to sustain flame; worthless.

Be prepared—there could be a situation where you feel as though you might as well be on the backside of the moon when it comes to a survival situation. Keep that positive mental attitude active and nurtured.

Appendix III

Further Reading

Special thanks to Buck Tilton, director of the Wilderness
Medicine Institute of the National Outdoor Leadership School,
author of Backcountry First Aid and Extended Care, 4th
Edition, published by Globe Pequot. It is included as the
official field reference in Atwater Carey medical kits. Mr. Tilton
is a well-respected and leading expert/author in this field. See
www.pharmacalway.com for more information.

Another great source of wilderness medicine information is *A
Comprehensive Guide to Wilderness and Travel Medicine*, by
Eric A. Weiss, M.D., published by Adventure Medical Kits. Dr.
Weiss's guide is included in all AMK kits. The guide features
handy and valuable excerpted tips, called "Weiss Advice,"
throughout its pages. See www.adventuremedicalkits.com.

Other references and just good reading: *Hypothermia: Death by
Exposure*, by Wm. W. Forgey, M.D. An excellent source of
information on hypothermia. Published by ICS Books, Inc.,
ISBN 0-934802-10-6.

*Alaska's Wilderness Medicines: Healthful Plants of the Far
North*, by Eleanor G. Viereck. Exacting uses of scores of plants
common not only in Alaska, but throughout at least the temperate range of North America. Published by Alaska Northwest
Books, ISBN 0-88240-322-2.

*Desperate Journeys, Abandoned Souls: True Stories of Cast-
aways and Other Survivors*, by Edward E. Leslie. Centuries of
harrowing survival tales from around the world. Published by
Mariner Books, Houghton Mifflin Company, ISBN 0-395-91150-
8 (paperback).

Handbook for Boys, the official manual of the Boy Scouts of America. My edition is a used, sixty-five cent, dog-eared, faded cover, hand-me-down—one of my most treasured books in my humble library. Originally printed in 1911, mine is the 5th edition from 1948. Hardly critical reading, but it sparked in me nearly fifty years of appreciation of its written and illustrated treasures and values. Check you local BSA council for availability of the most current edition.

98.6 Degrees: The Art of Keeping Your Ass Alive! by Cody Lundin. One of the best books on the mental and physical aspects of survival on the market. I discuss many similar topics. I found his to be the one book I could relate to the most. Published by Gibbs-Smith Press, ISBN 1-58685-234-5.

AUTHOR ACKNOWLEDGMENTS

I spent a great many weekends during the summers of my youth roaming the hills and woods of east-central Missouri on camping trips with my family. Each camping trip with my dad or uncle was a learning experience in outdoor skills that has stayed with me all my life.

Later, in the Boy Scouts, working my way toward becoming an Eagle Scout, I learned even more skills and better ways of performing them. My scoutmaster, Doug "Mr. B." Barkley, also taught me the values associated with each skill and helped me expand my thought processes. He taught me teamwork and shared responsibility with my fellow scouts. And he helped me to know what it means to "Be prepared!"

Pursuing a degree in forestry in Minnesota enabled me to expand my love and understanding of the outdoors. Dr. "Scotty" Scholten taught me how to identify nearly everything that grew in the wild. I learned how everything is tied together, how the ecology, geology, climate and other factors come together to give a region its character and personality.

I spent almost 20 years living in Alaska. As the owner/operator and guide of a sea kayak touring business and as a volunteer with the local Search and Rescue unit on Kodiak Island (where we had the benefit of the knowledge of the local U.S. Navy Seals training unit stationed there), I honed my skills to be better prepared for any situations that might arise from the deathly cold and unforgiving environment of the North Pacific region.

And to the best traveling partner a backpacker or kayaker could have, Craig Swedberg, thanks for pulling me back up onto the Inca Trail that one rainy and windy night high above the Urubamba River in Peru. You've made every outdoor adventure a grand, humorous and truly pleasurable experience.

To everyone connected with the outdoors—resource people, SAR teams and others—thank you for what you do so well!

— Tom Watson, 2006

INDEX

A

Abdomen, 153
Airway passages, 149
Anger, 26
Anxiety, 20
Artificial flints, 112
Assessing injuries, 148, 151
Assessing the survival mode, 14–27
Audible signals, 131

B

Bandage, 157
Beaches, 86
Bites, 156, 172
Bivy sack, 46
Bleeding, 150, 157, 160
Blisters, 158
Body parts at risk, 153
Bowline knot, 68
Breathing, 149
Broken bones, 159
Broken wrist challenge, 15
Building a fire, 102–119
Burns, 159, 160

C

Carbohydrates, 90
Care of fire, 119
Charts, 136
Chest, 154
Circumstances, 14
Clothing, 28–41
Clove hitch knot, 68
Compass, 138
Consciousness, 150
Cordage, 66

D

Dehydration, 75, 77, 161, 170
Dental problems, 160
Depression, 22, 23
Desert shelter, 63
Developing navigation skills, 136–145
Dew, 81
Don't wander, 132
Drowning, 164

E

Elements of survival, 6
Emotions, 19
Equipment bag, 41
Equipment failures, 16
Eyeglasses, 168

F

Fat, 90
Fatigue, 25
Fear, 20
Feet Warmer, 40
Figure 8 knot, 69
Finding water, 74–87
Fire starters, 108–116
    Artificial flints, 112
    Flint and steel, 112
    Friction method, 114
    Lenses, 115
    Lighters, 113
    Magnesium starter kits, 112
    Magnifying glasses, 115
    Matches, 109
Fire, 102–119
First aid, 146–179
Fish, 97
Flint and steel, 112

Food, 88–101
Footgear, 32
Friction method, 114
Frostbite, 161
Fuel, 105

G

Gaiters, 35
Game birds, 99
Gear, 28–53
Geography, 17
Global positioning system, 140
Go "undercover," 59
Guilt, 23

H

Half hitch knot, 69
Hammock, 50
Head, 154
Heat exhaustion, 162, 170
Heat stroke, 162
Herbal therapies, 22
Hobo fire, 119
How to build, 65–72
Hunter's fire, 118
Hyponatremia, 163
Hypothermia, 163

I

Ice, 85
Infection, 165
Insects, 98

K

Kindling, 107
Knife, 50
Knots, 68
Know your signals, 125

L

Lashing, 70–72
Lean-to, 60

Lenses, 115
Lighters, 113
Log cabin fire, 117
Long fire, 117
Lost on the moon test, 29

M

Magnesium starter kits, 112
Magnifying glasses, 115
Makeshift mirror, 52
Making signals, 120–135
Mammals, 100
Maps, 136
Matches, 109
Mechanical failures, 16
Medical conditions, 20
Medical emergencies, 155
Medicinal plant remedies, 176
Mind aids, 26
Minerals, 90
Morse code, 124
Multi-use equipment, 52

N

Natural remedies, 176
Navigation, 136–145
Neck, 155
Nine rules of survival, 11
Nutrient needs, 89–91
Nylon stocking, 16

O

Overview of gear, 28–53

P

Panic attack, 21
Personal locator beacons, 132
Plant moisture, 82
Plants, 91–97, 176
Poncho, 46
Prioritizing, 6
Protein, 90

Pyramid fire, 117

R

Rabies, 165
Rainwater, 81
Reflector fire, 118
Roof options, 73

S

Sea, 86
Search and rescue, 142
Searching for food, 88–101
Seven steps to survival, 8
Sheer lash, 71
Sheet bend knot, 69
Shelter vent, 60
Shelter ventilation, 63
Shock, 151
Signal fire, 119
Signals, 120–135
Sleeping bag, 42–46
Sleeping pad, 47
Snakebite, 166
Snow, 85
  Shelter, 61
  Walls, 62
Socks, 33
Solar still, 83
Special tips for children, 12
Spinal damage, 152
Splint, 167
Sprains, 166
Square lash, 71
Square/reef knot, 68
Star fire, 117
Stings, 156, 172
Strains, 166
Stress, 24

T

Tautline hitch knot, 69
Tent, 48

Timber hitch knot, 69
Tinder, 106
Tipi fire, 116
Tourniquet, 158
Trail marker, 144
Trench and pit fires, 118
Types of fire, 116–119
  Hobo fire, 119
  Hunter's fire, 118
  Log cabin fire, 117
  Long fire, 117
  Pyramid/crisscross fire, 117
  Reflector fire, 118
  Signal fire, 119
  Star fire, 117
  Tipi fire, 116
  Trench and pit fires, 118

V

Vision problems, 167
Visual signals, 120–130
  Bright colors, 122
  Fire, 125
  Flare, 128
  Ground signals, 123
  Hand and arm signals, 126
  Lights, 130
  Mirror, 126
  Shiny objects, 122
  Smoke, 130
Vitamins, 90

W

Water Filter, 34
Water, 74–87
Weather, 16
What to build, 59–65
When to build, 58
Where to build, 56
Wood, 108
Wound, 153, 169

Creative Publishing international
is your complete source of How-to information for the Outdoors.

Available Outdoor Titles:

Hunting Books
* Advanced Turkey Hunting
* Advanced Whitetail Hunting
* Bowhunting Equipment & Skills
* The Complete Guide to Hunting
* Dog Training
* Duck Hunting
* Elk Hunting
* Hunting Record-Book Bucks
* Mule Deer Hunting
* Muzzleloading
* Pronghorn Hunting
* Whitetail Hunting
* Whitetail Techniques & Tactics
* Wild Turkey

Fishing Books
* Advanced Bass Fishing
* The Art of Freshwater Fishing
* The Complete Guide to Freshwater Fishing
* Fishing for Catfish
* Fishing Rivers & Streams
* Fishing Tips & Tricks
* Fishing with Artificial Lures
* Inshore Salt Water Fishing
* Kids Gone Fishin'
* Largemouth Bass
* Live Bait Fishing
* Modern Methods of Ice Fishing
* Northern Pike & Muskie
* Offshore Salt Water Fishing
* Panfish
* Salt Water Fishing Tactics

* Smallmouth Bass
* Striped Bass Fishing: Salt Water Strategies
* Successful Walleye Fishing
* Trout
* Ultralight Fishing

Fly Fishing Books
* The Art of Fly Tying
* The Art of Fly Tying – CD ROM
* Fishing Dry Flies – Surface Presentations for Trout in Streams
* Fishing Nymphs, Wet Flies & Streamers – Subsurface Techniques for Trout in Streams
* Fly-Fishing Equipment & Skills
* Fly Fishing for Beginners
* Fly Fishing for Trout in Streams
* Fly-Tying Techniques & Patterns

Cookbooks
* America's Favorite Fish Recipes
* America's Favorite Wild Game Recipes
* Babe & Kris Winkelman's Great Fish & Game Recipes
* Backyard Grilling
* Cooking Wild in Kate's Camp
* Cooking Wild in Kate's Kitchen
* Dressing & Cooking Wild Game
* Game Bird Cookery
* The New Cleaning & Cooking Fish
* Preparing Fish & Wild Game
* The Saltwater Cookbook
* Venison Cookery

To purchase these or other Creative Publishing international titles, contact your local bookseller, or visit our website at **www.creativepub.com**